Fifty Figure Drawings

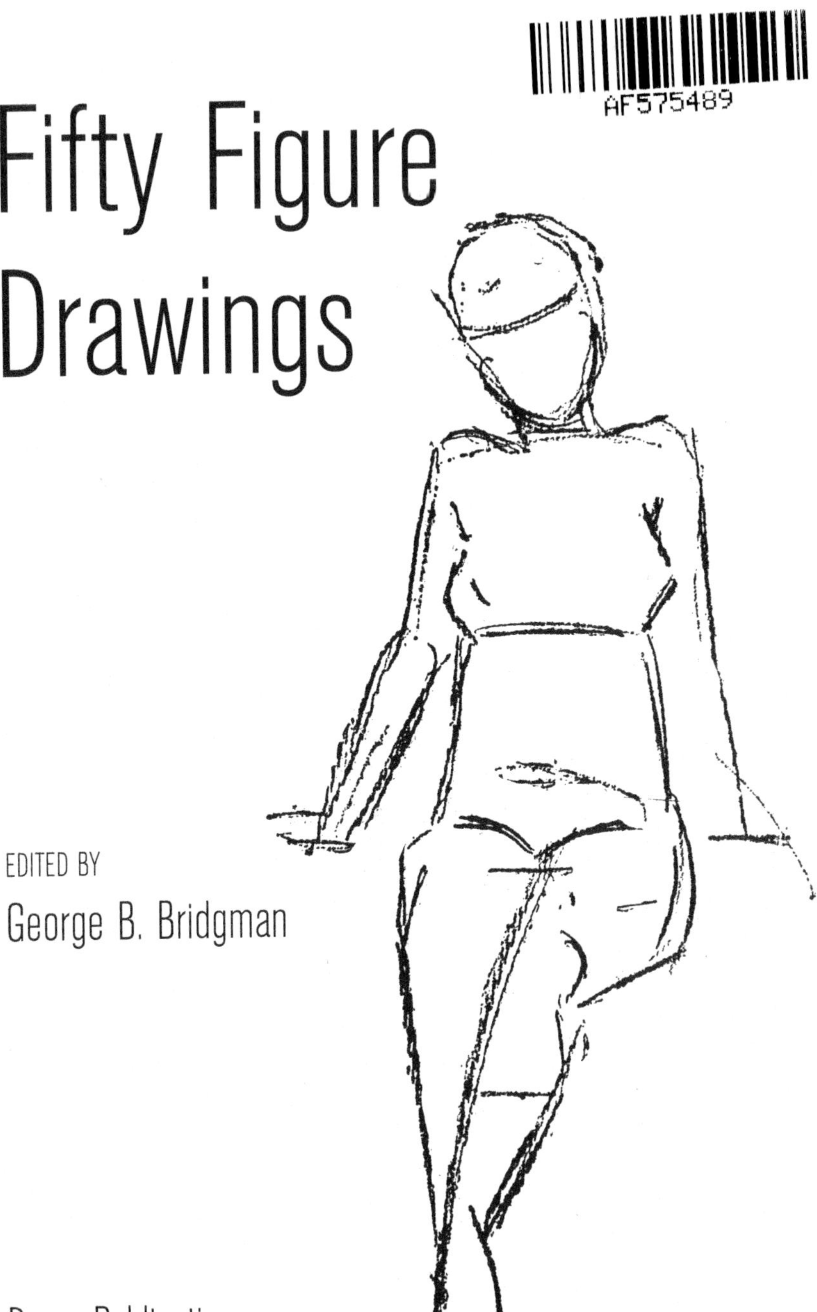

EDITED BY

George B. Bridgman

Dover Publications
Garden City, New York

Bibliographical Note

This Dover edition, first published in 2006, is an unabridged republication of the 1937 sixth printing, revised edition, of the work originally published by Bridgman Publishers Inc., Pelham, New York, in 1927.

Library of Congress Cataloging-in-Publication Data

Fifty figure drawings / edited by George B. Bridgman.
p. cm.
Unabridged republication of the 1937 rev. ed. of the work originally published: New York : Bridgman Publishers, 1927.
ISBN-13: 978-0-486-45120-6 (pbk.)
ISBN-10: 0-486-45120-8 (pbk.)
1. Figure drawing. 2. Human figure in art. I. Bridgman, George Brant, 1864-1943.

NC765.F45 2006
743.4—dc22

2006046291

Manufactured in the United States by LSC Communications Book LLC
45120804 2021
www.doverpublications.com

Foreword

THE purpose of this book is to show by definite examples the best work produced by students of the leading Art Schools of this country. It is in fact a summary of International Life Class work, making apparent the different styles, technique, creative power and artistic expression of the human figure. In producing this book, we hope that it will forward and benefit the art student for self training in drawing, by understanding, studying and analyzing various phases of draftsmanship developing at the present time. This book is full of progressive suggestions and important facts, practical to both the instructor and the student. To those who have so liberally furnished the many fine drawings reproduced herewith for publication, we express our appreciation and thanks.

The Publishers

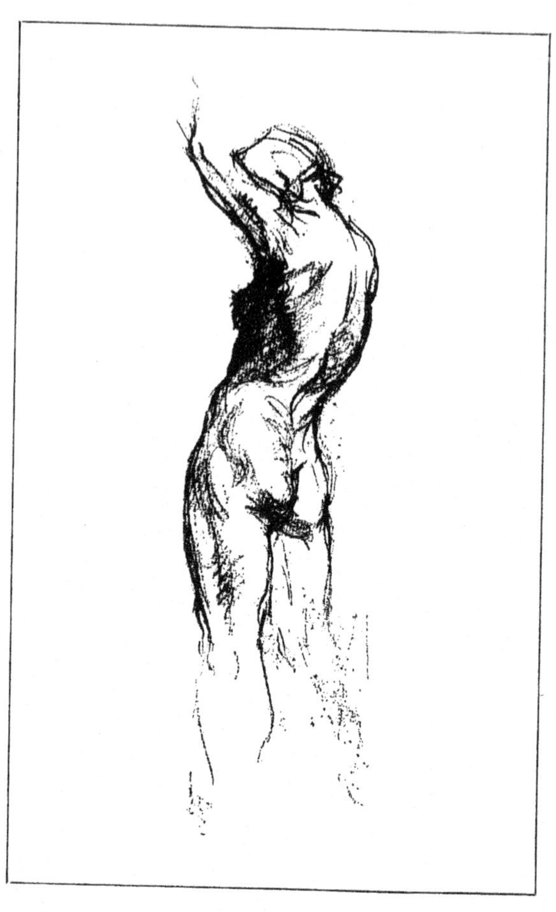

FIFTY FIGURE DRAWINGS

IN EUROPE the art schools of the past consisted of groups of workmen held together by a master Director, much as is today, the commercial art studio, where there is directing head, or a modern master who corresponds in a modern sense to the old masters of the past.

In the studio of Peter Paul Reubens the apprentice student worked on and carried out the conceptions of the master and at one time there were as many as one hundred student helpers or apprentices working in his Antwerp Studio. Van Dyck had his London school and Rembrandt a school at Antwerp. The training apprentices today come from the art school.

In America we have had no artistic tradition, we have borrowed only from what has been done before. The old apprentice school is in modern American way, Art School of today. The schools and the classes are patterned very much after the schools of Europe in a general way, but the policies vary greatly. Instructors naturally have many different viewpoints, regarding artistic training and instruction. A great number of Life Class instructors have had their training in European schools and have incorporated into their methods, modern European traditions. It must be taken into consideration that we have here a nation of many races and creeds varying greatly in ideals and tastes, material and artistic. Due somewhat to an ever changing commercial influence the manner of instruction changes continually, which, in itself, becomes a development in keeping with our needs. It will be seen in the following pages many phases and influences of draftsmanship, in some cases separate, and in others interwoven, but to the discerning eye the drawings selected can be classified under three different trends of thought, the imitative, the constructive, and the expressive.

Imitative art is the basic language of pictorial writing, in writing, ideas are expressed with pictured objects representing something, seen or heard. Writing originated in drawing. Letters were our first pictures, so, to express oneself, one must imitate.

Constructive drawing is built upon the fact that there are three great masses of the human body, made up of, the head, the chest and the pelvis. To give the expression of movement these masses must tilt, turn, or twist. If the masses change, the outline changes, giving a sense of balance. You have, the principles of construction.

To express one's innerself so that others can understand you, is art. If your expressions are elevated and beautiful it is good art, this is the basis of our third classification. Expressive.

To convey ideas in writing one must learn to write, in art to convey ideas in paint one must learn how to use paint. The Language must be studied and expression encouraged. It is hoped that the absence of critical text will tend and encourage a serious study of the many fine drawings exhibited and that they will stimulate interest and offer many suggestions to both instructor and students.

CONTENTS

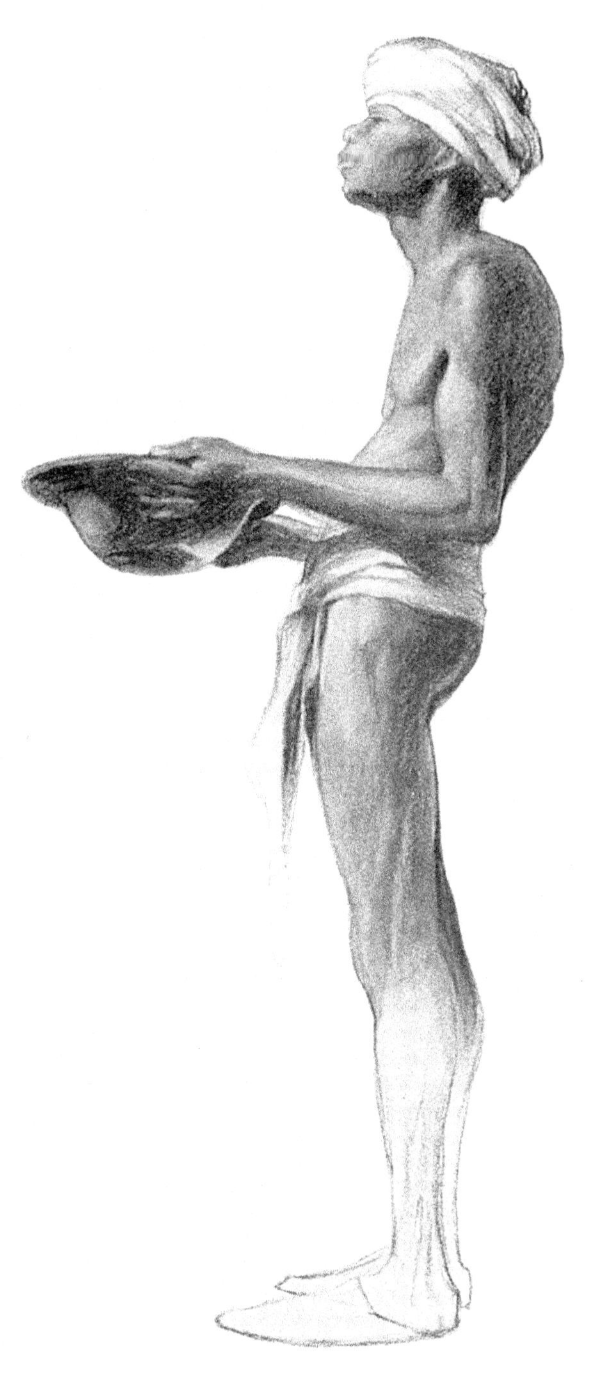

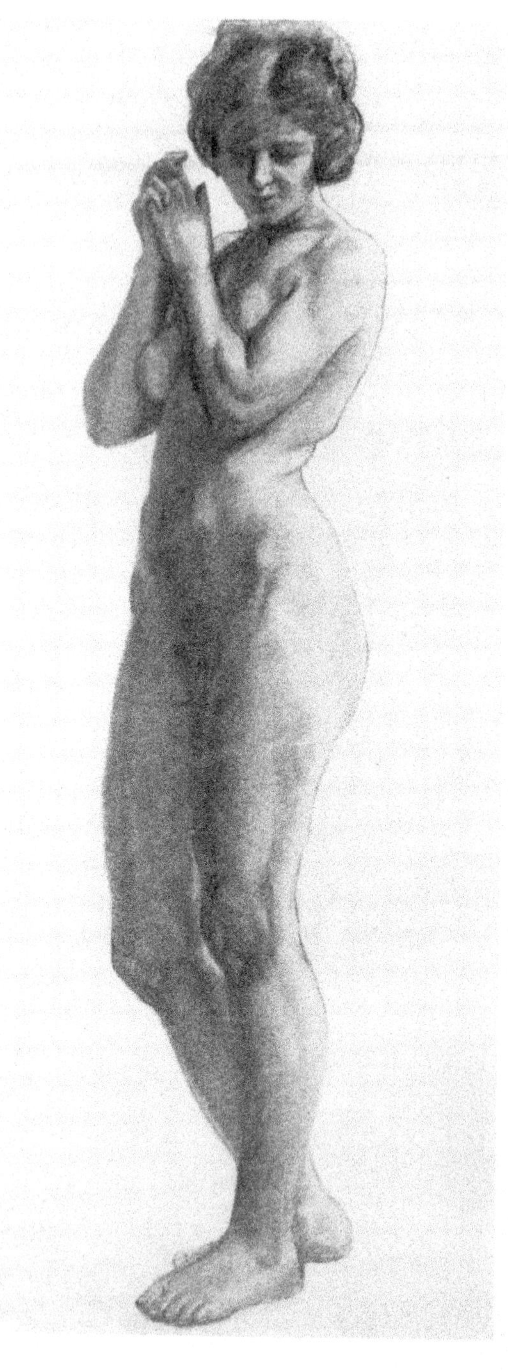

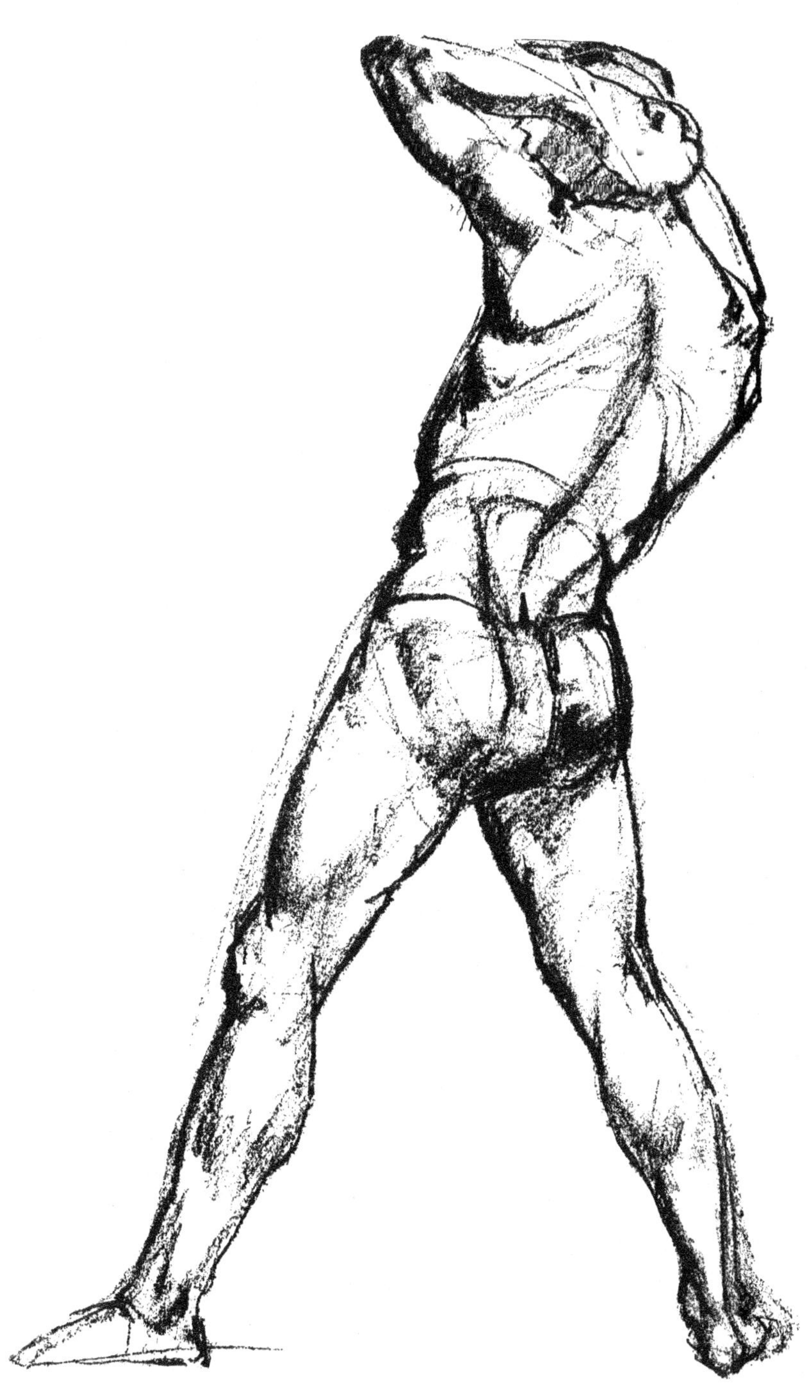

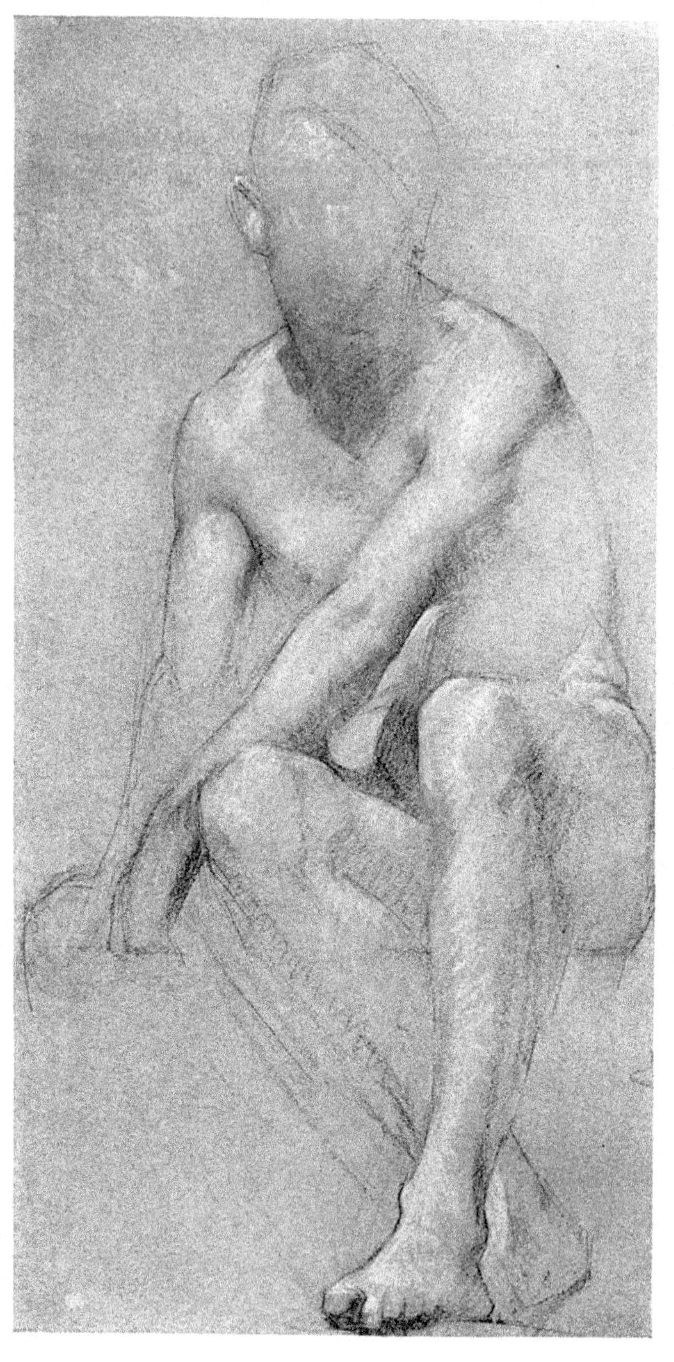

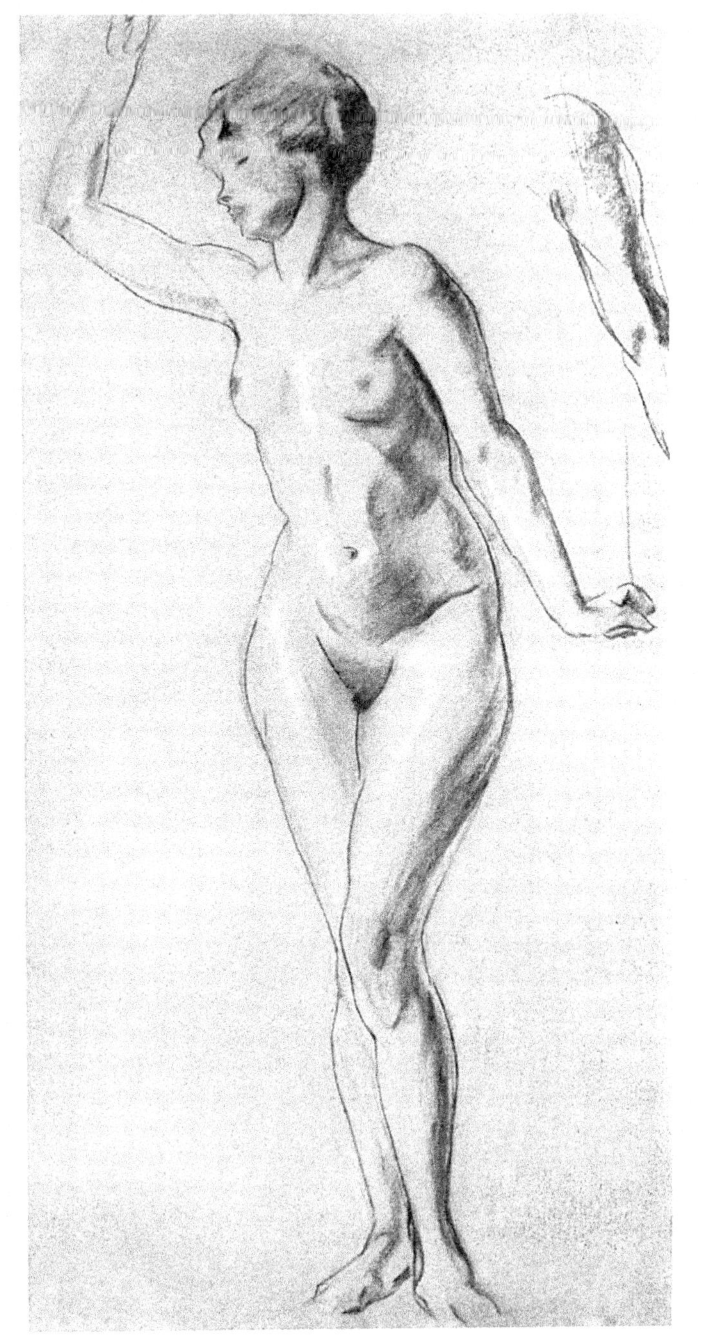

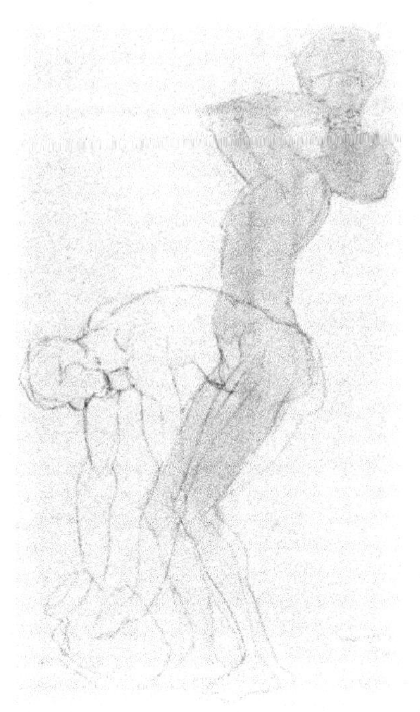

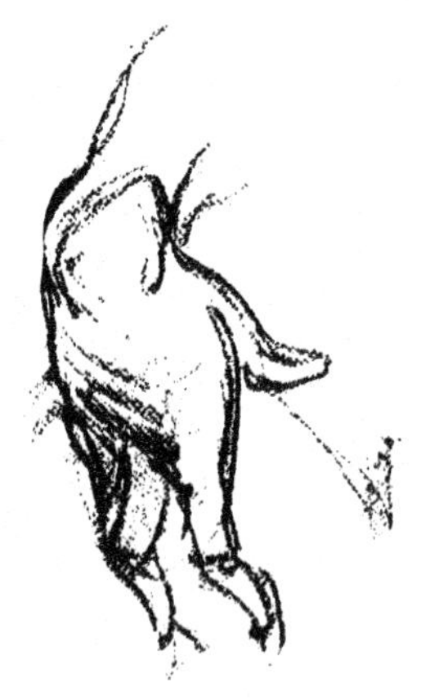

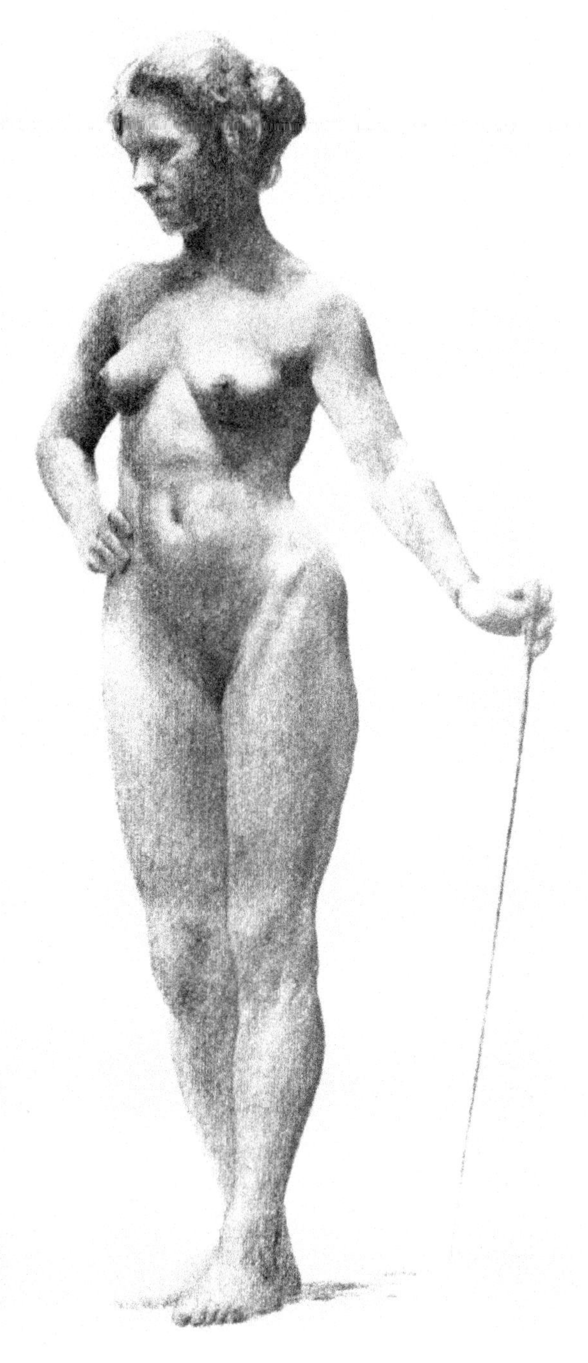

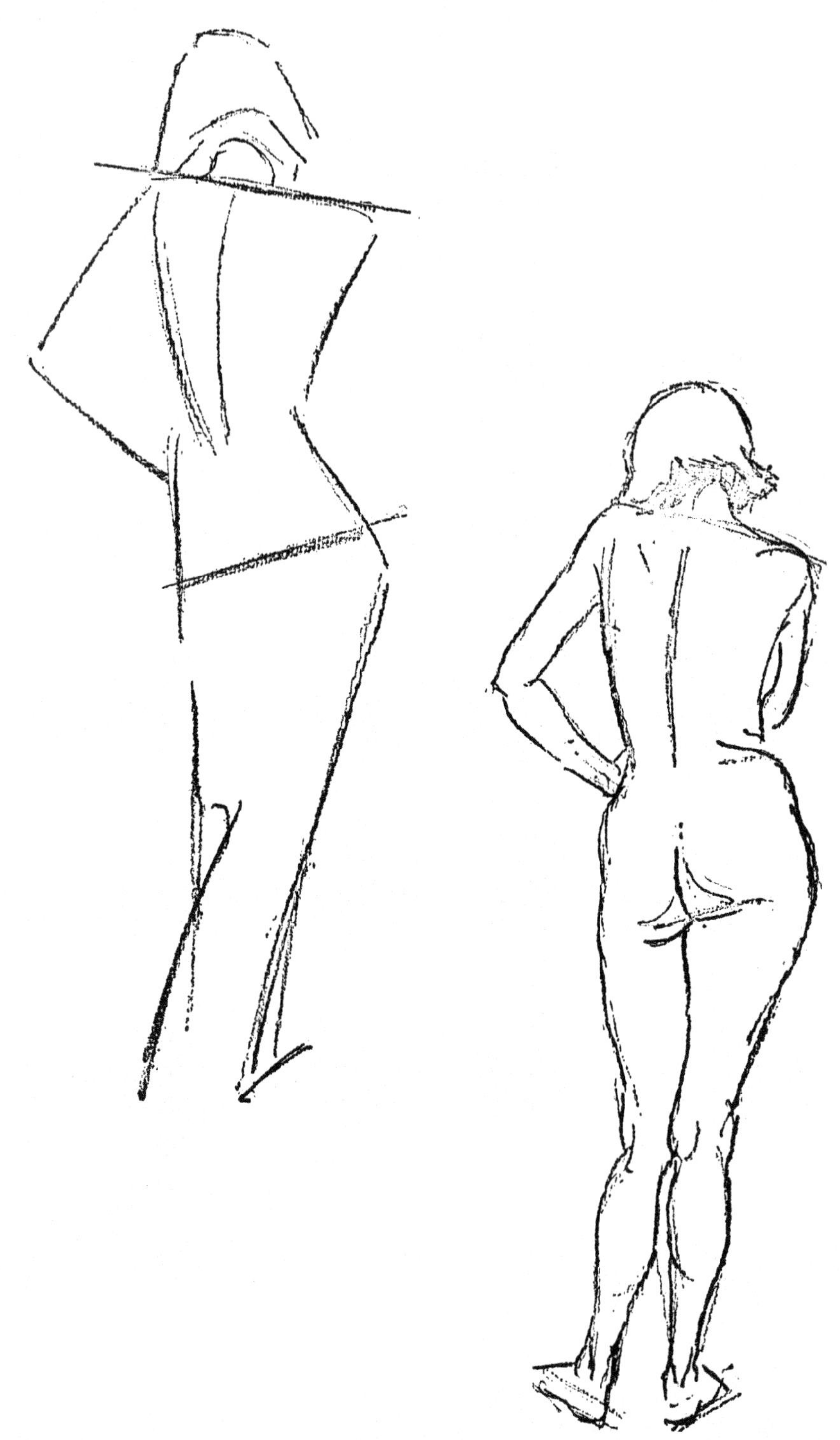

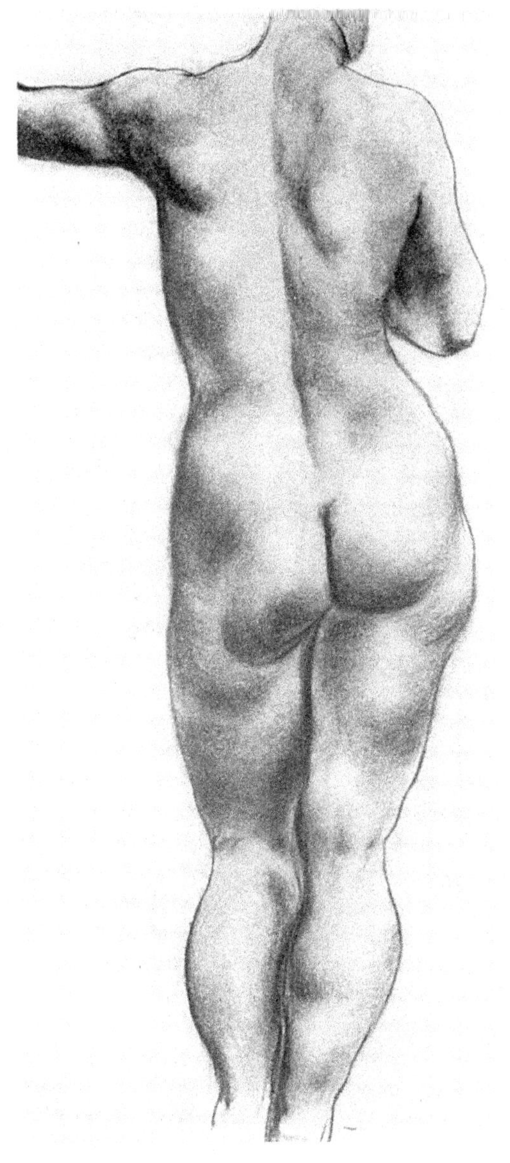

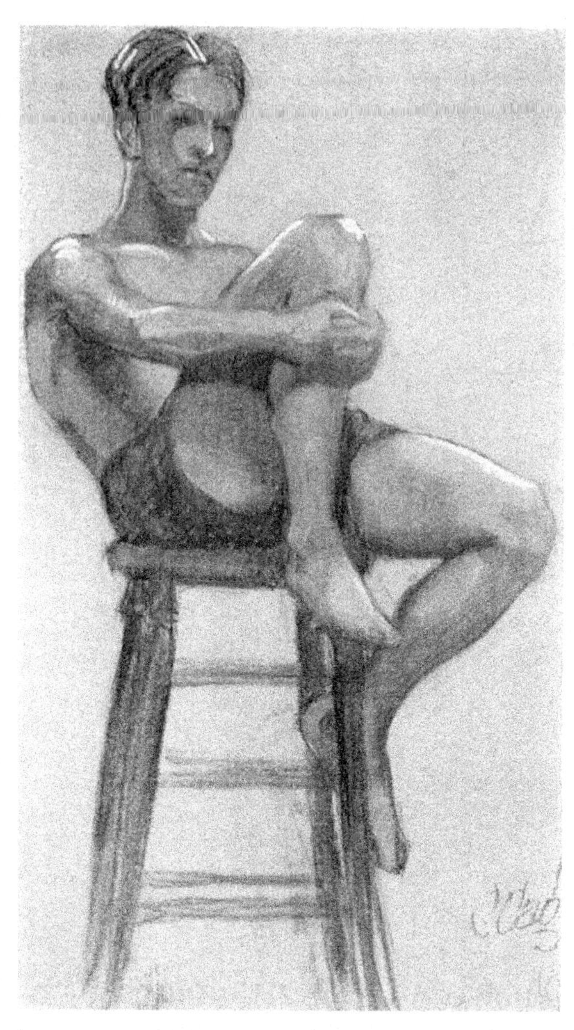

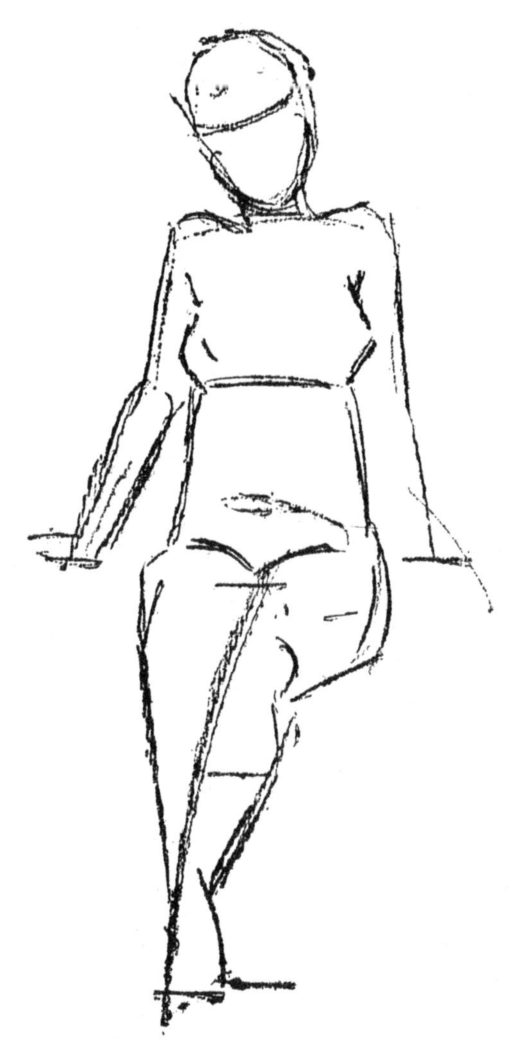

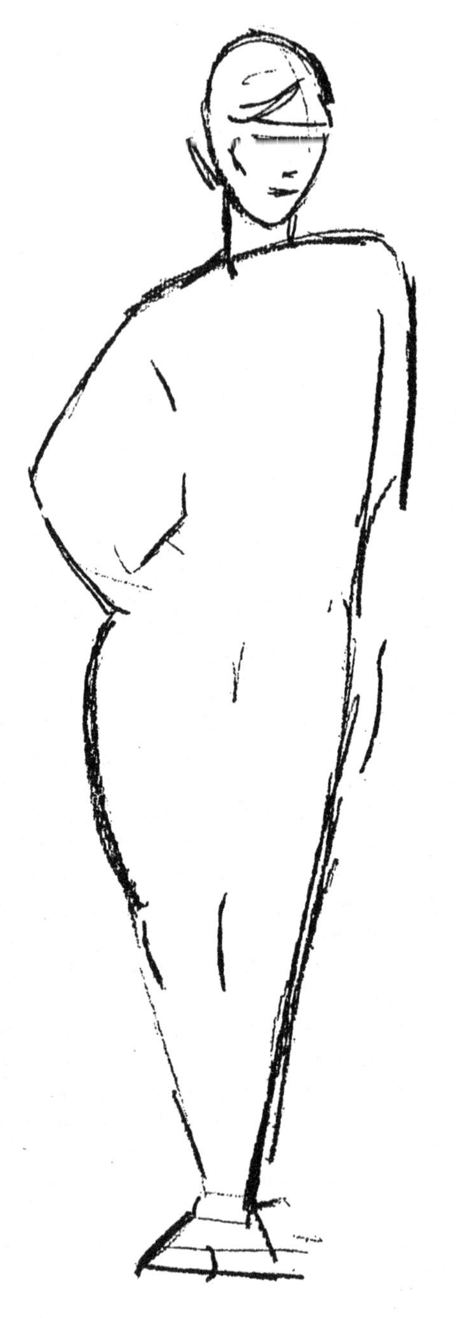

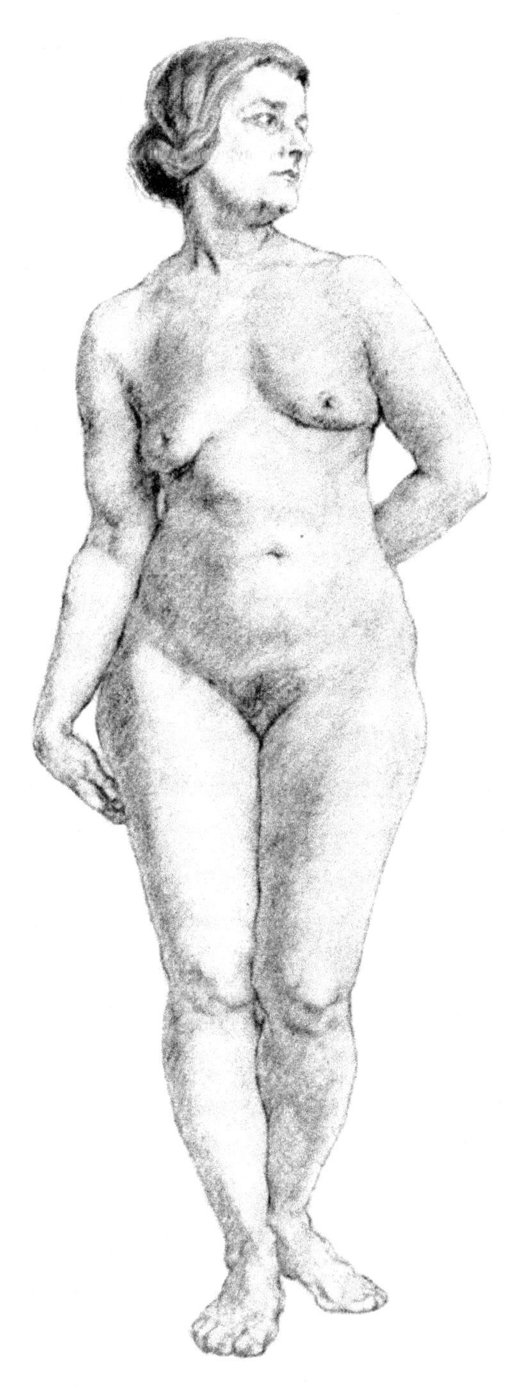

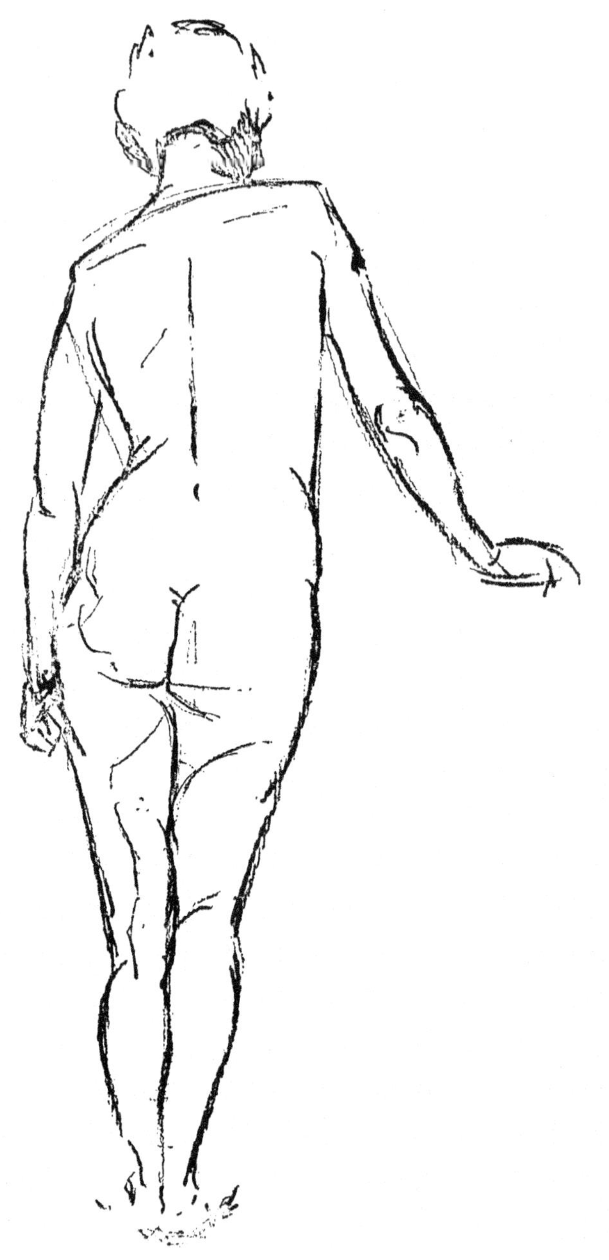

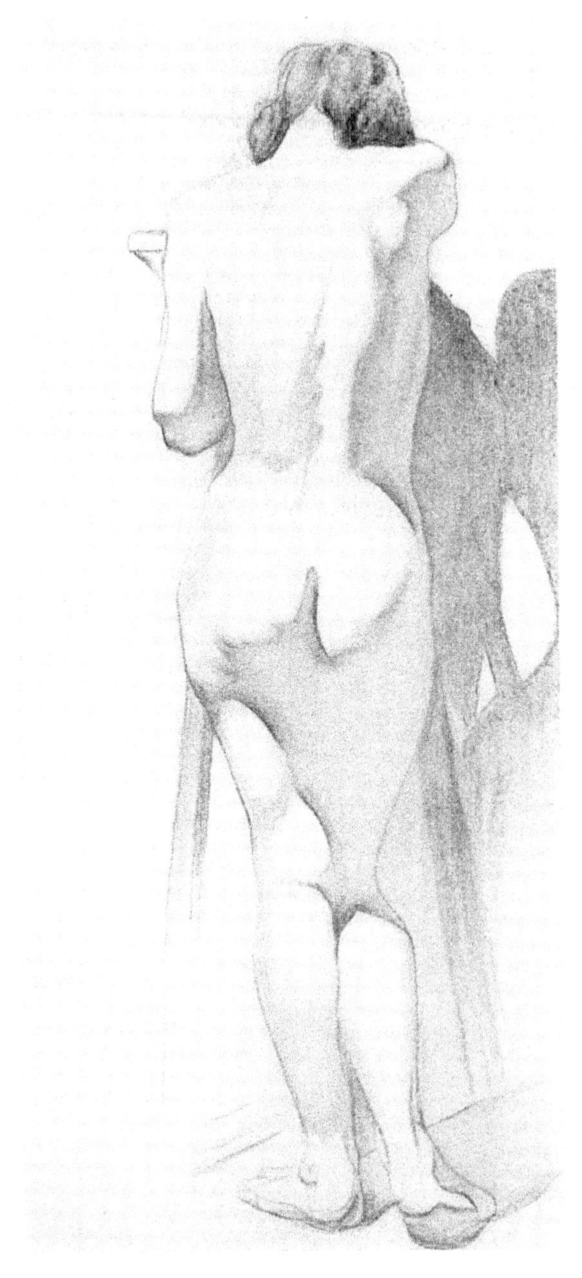

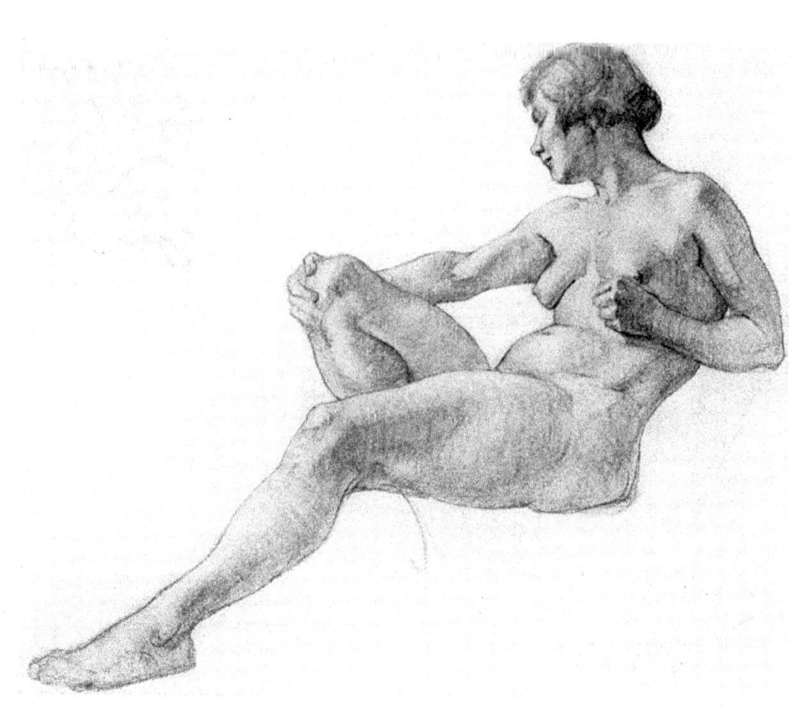

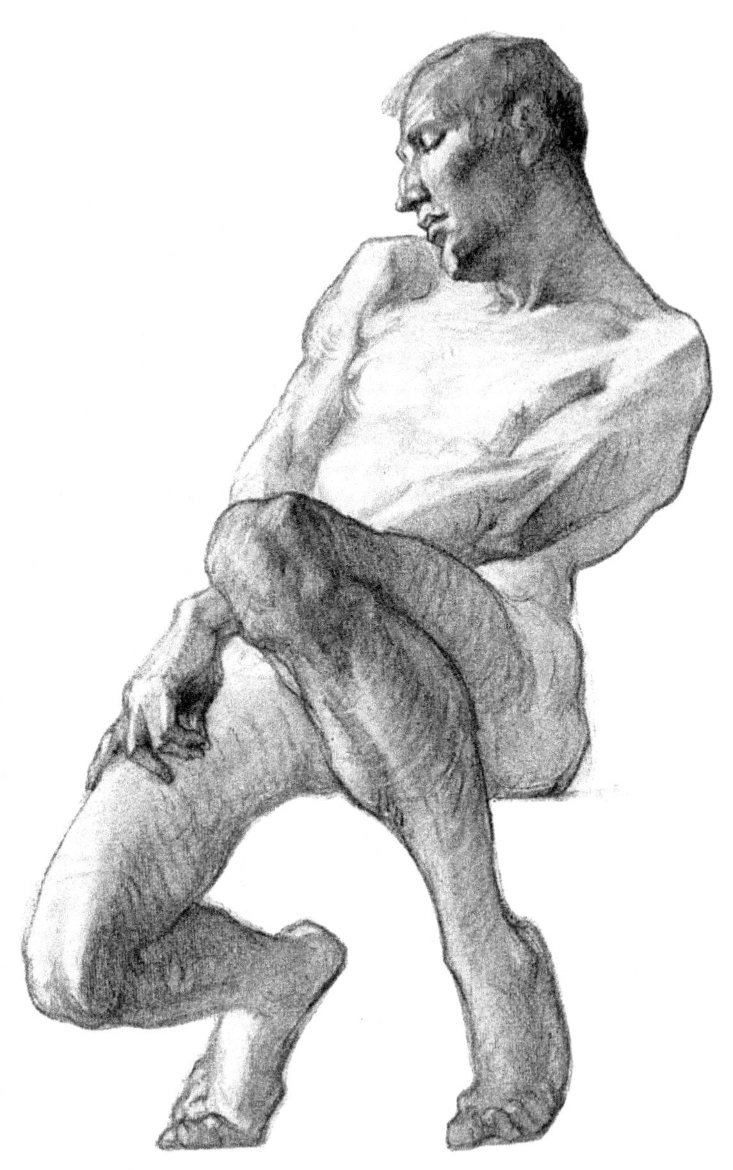

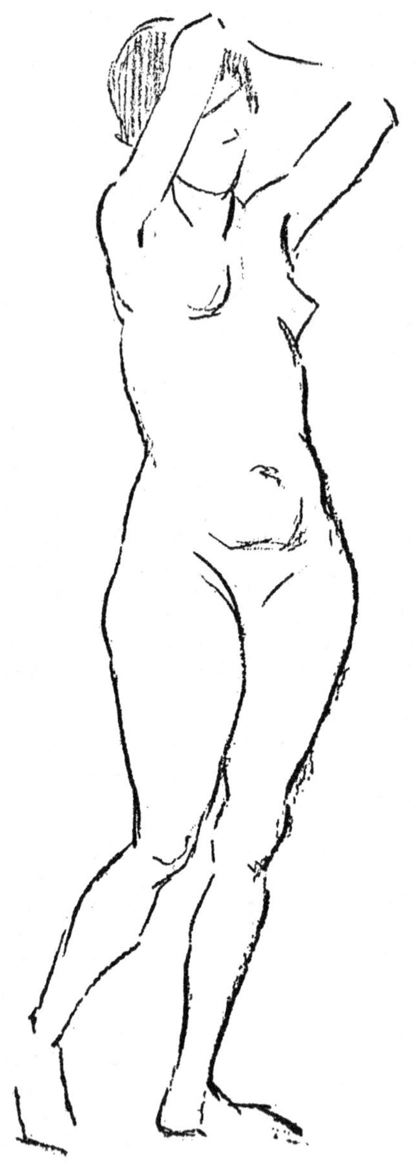

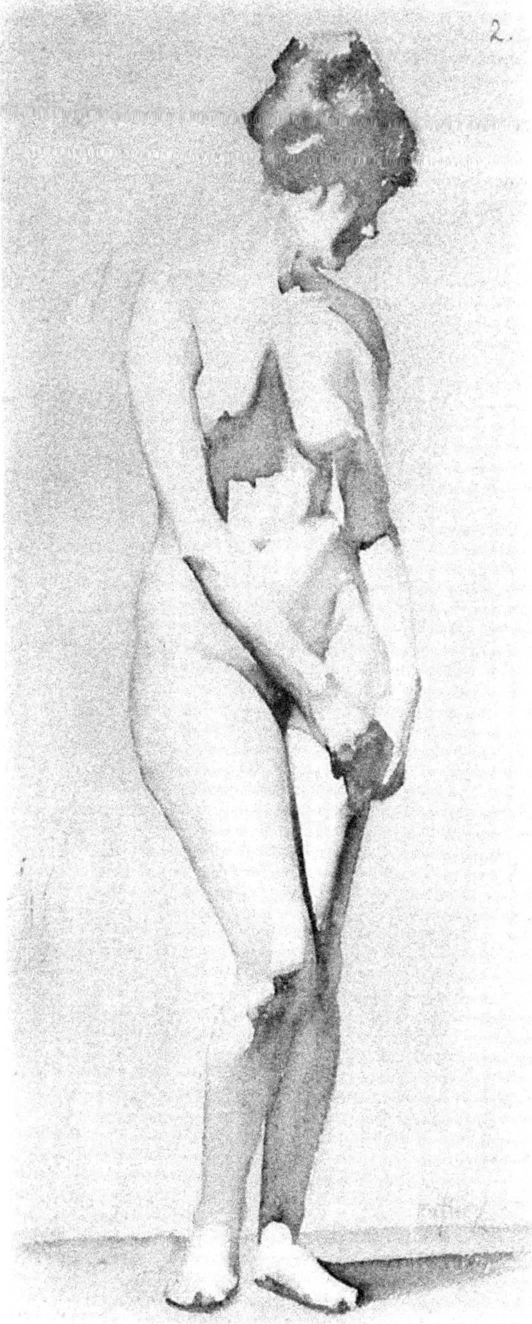

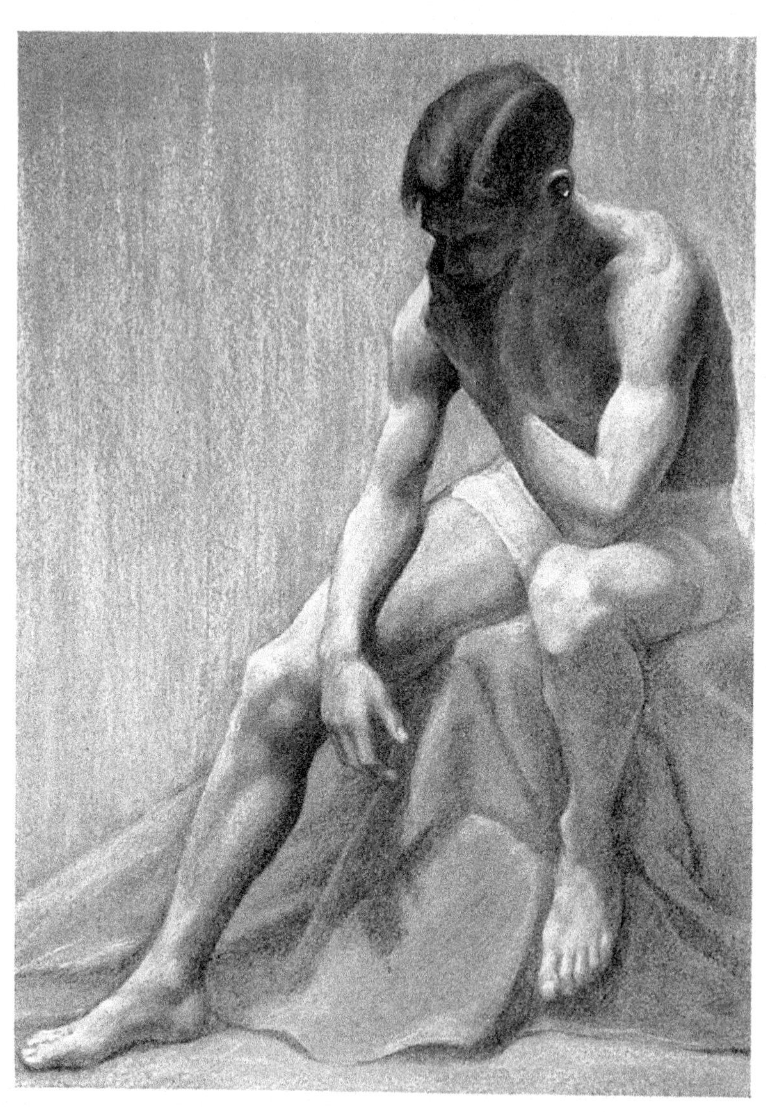

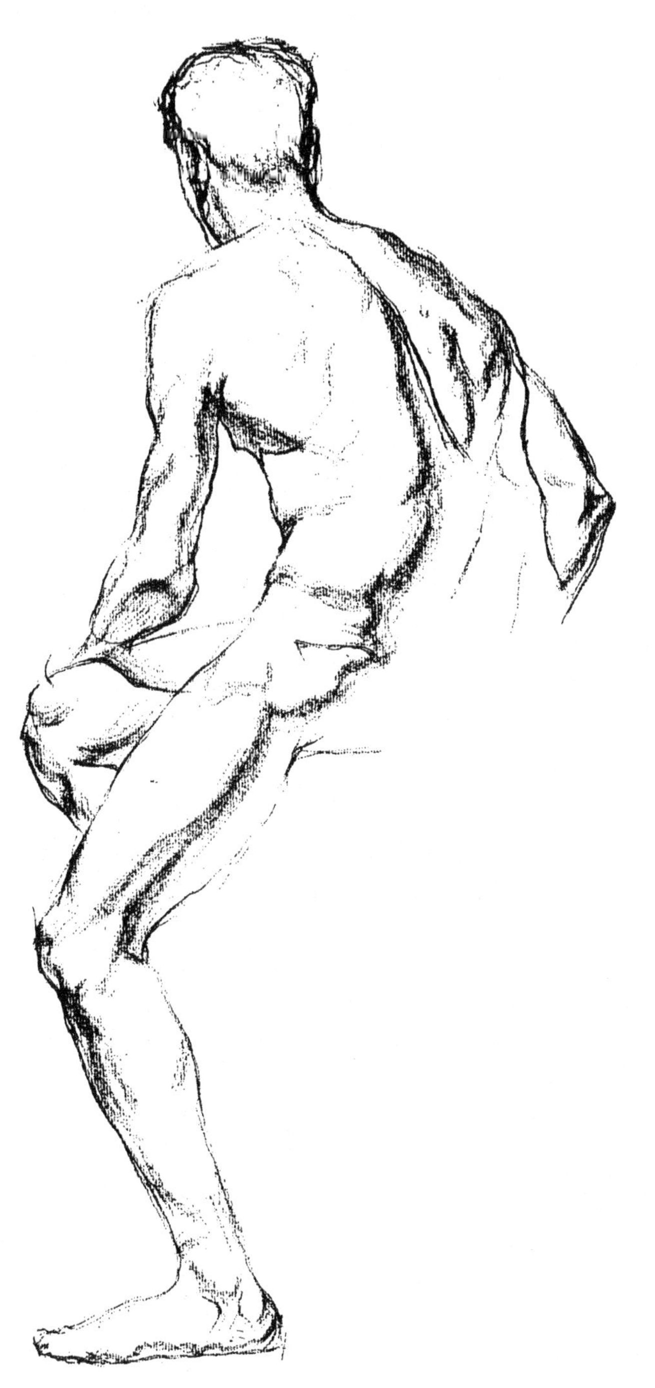

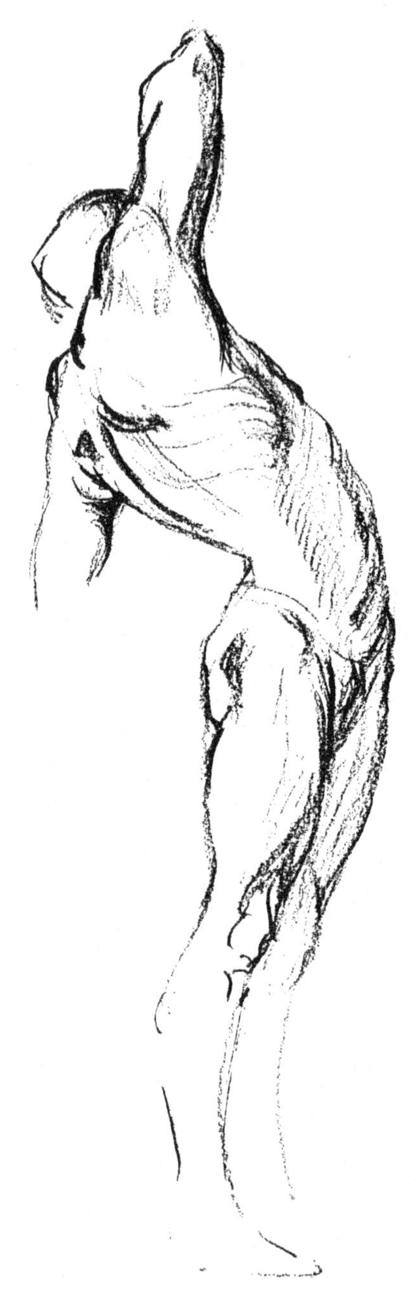

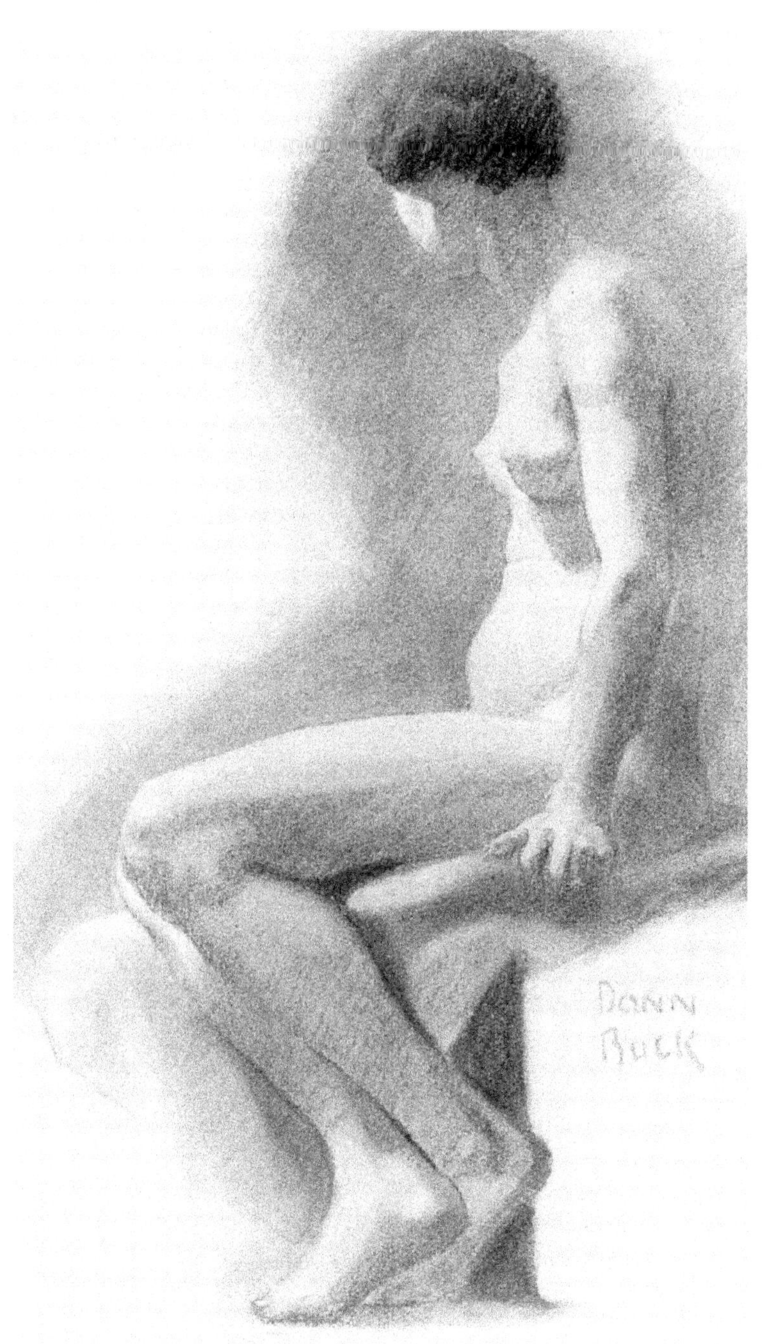
DONN
BUCK

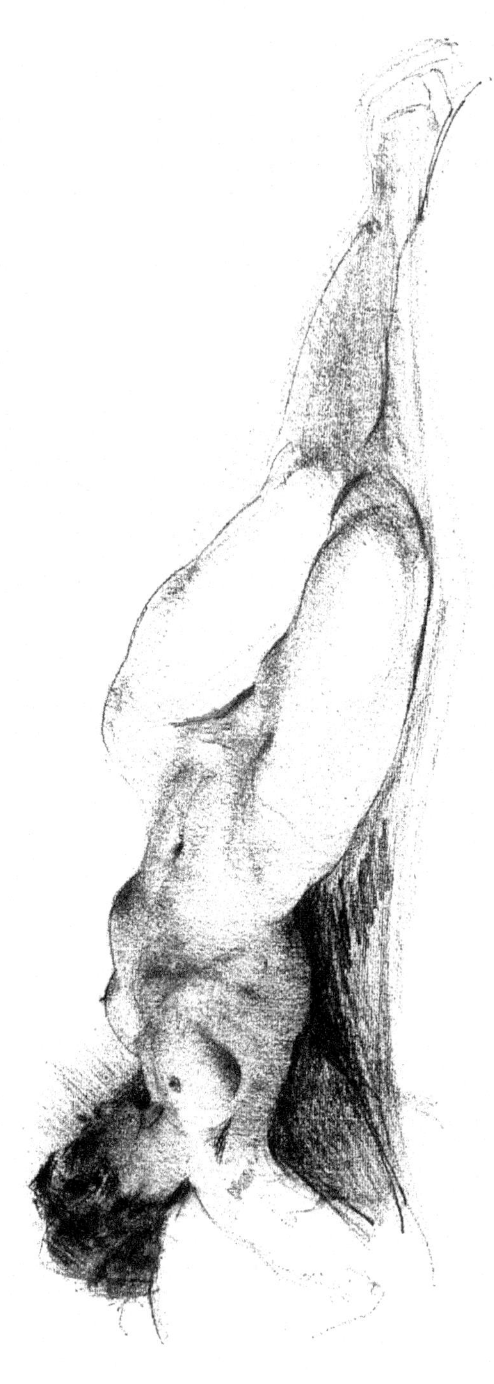

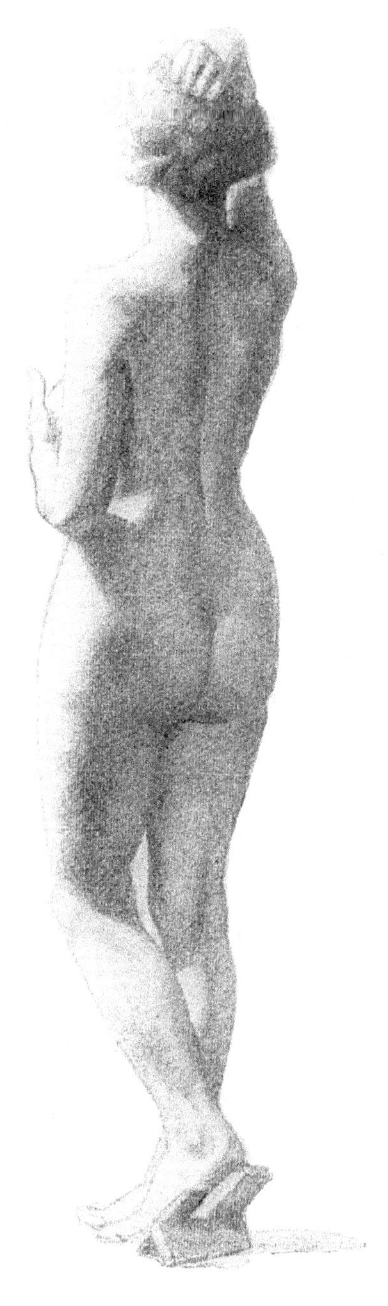

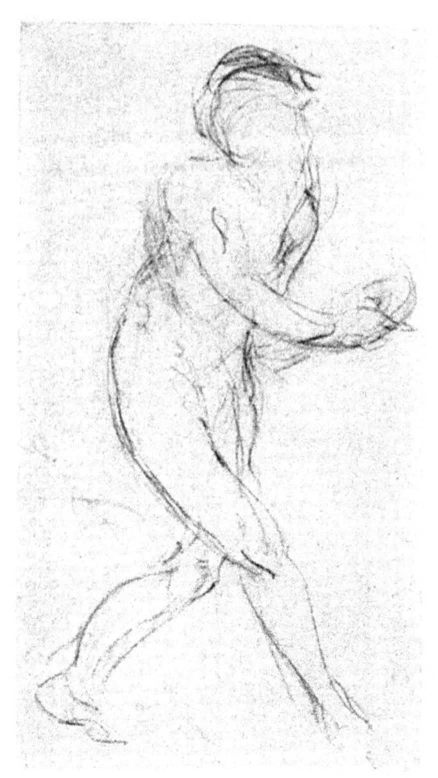

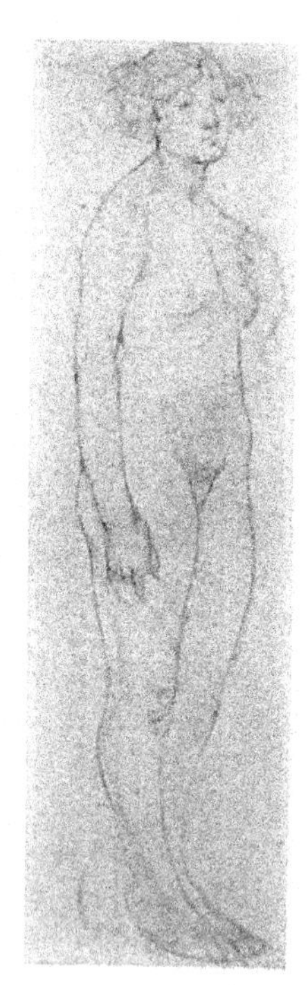

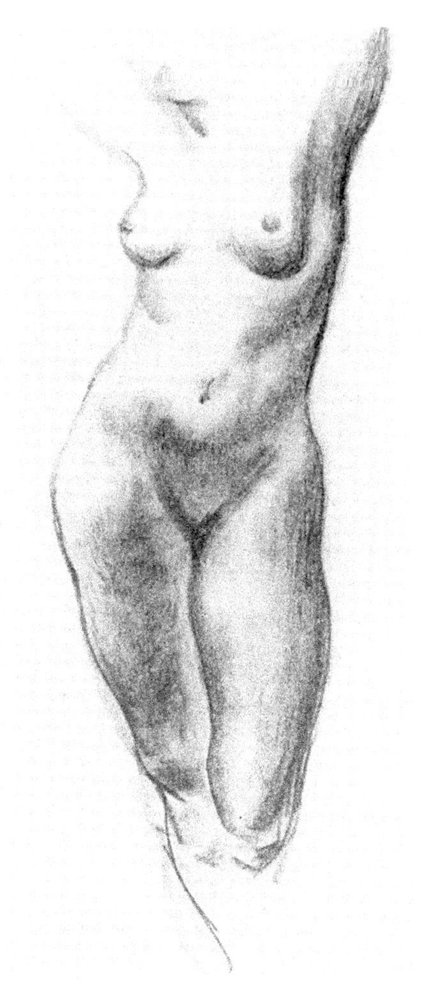

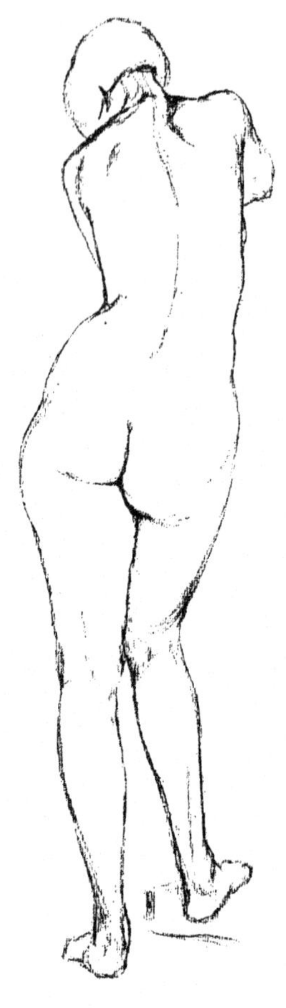

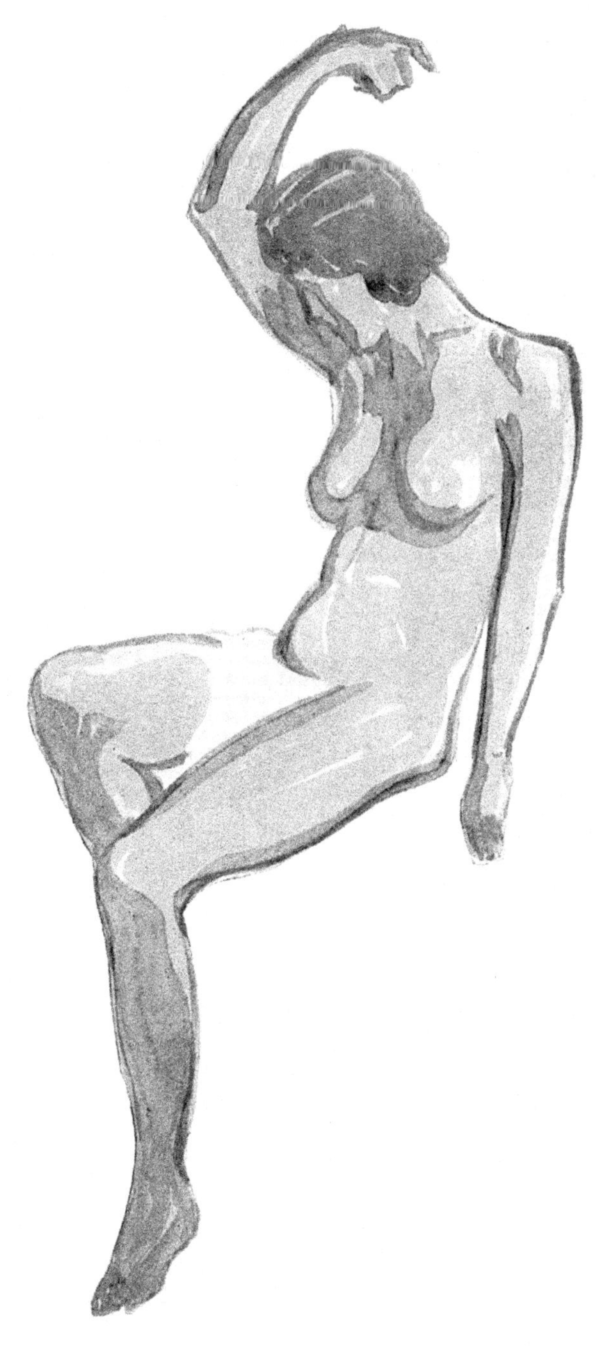

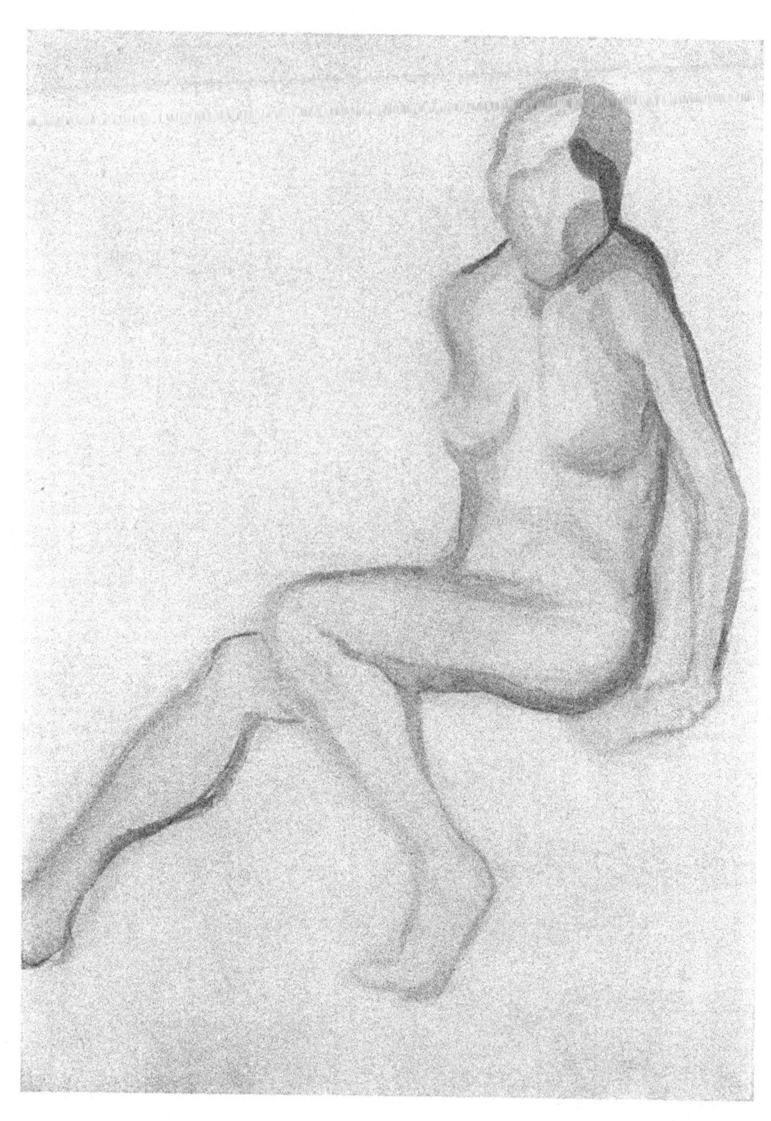

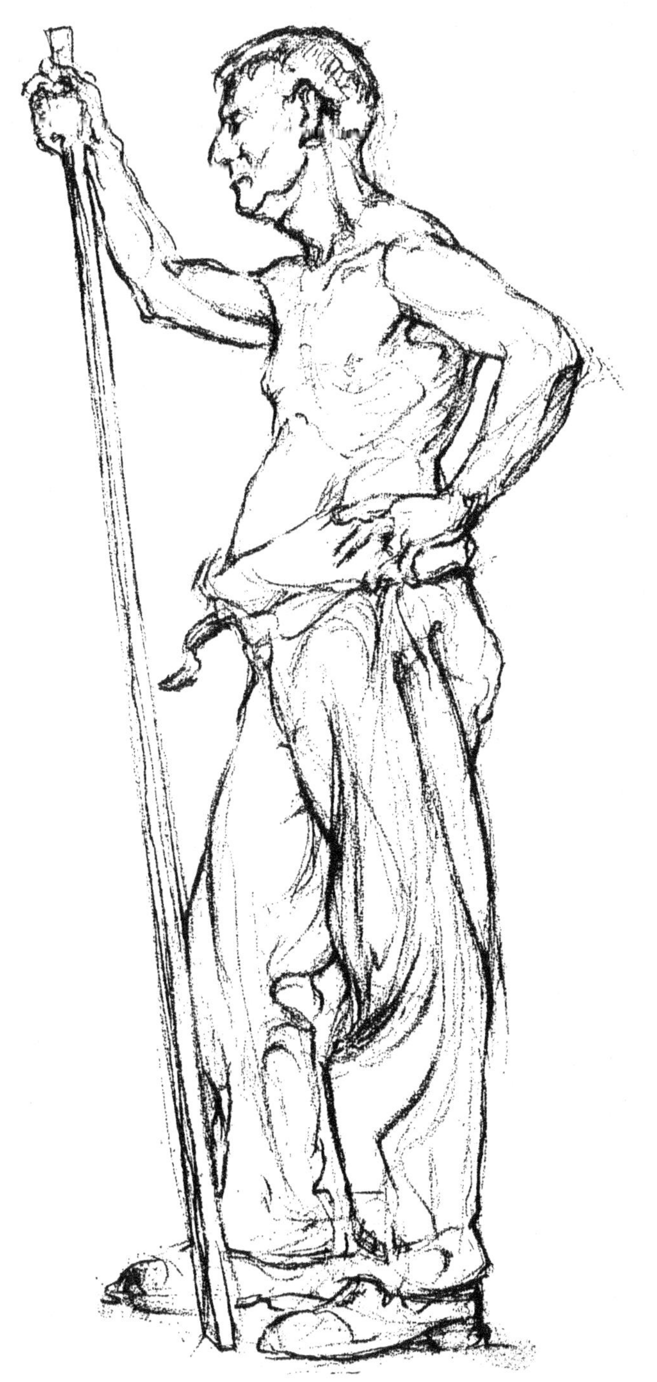

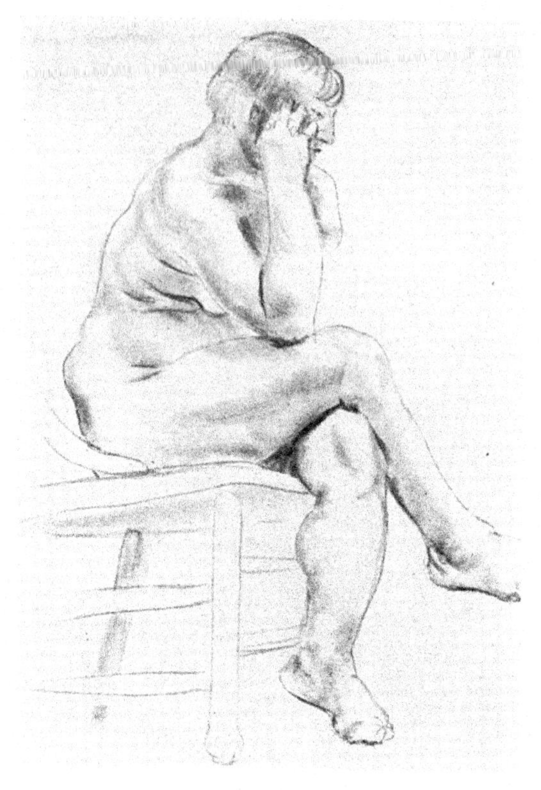

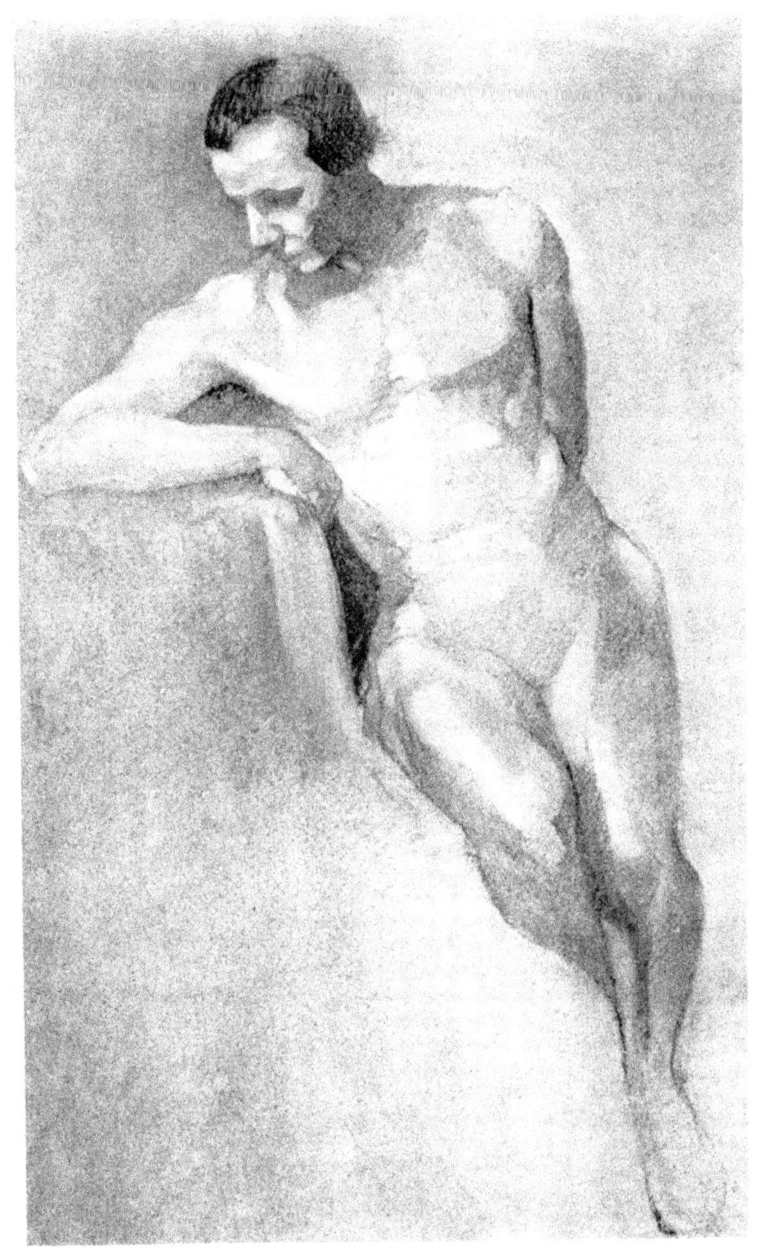

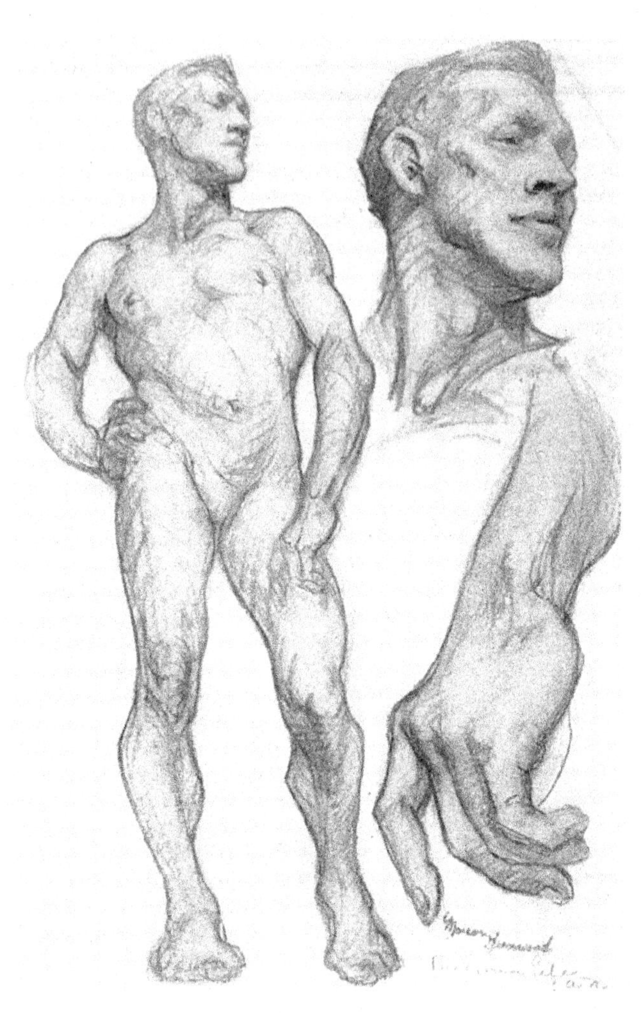

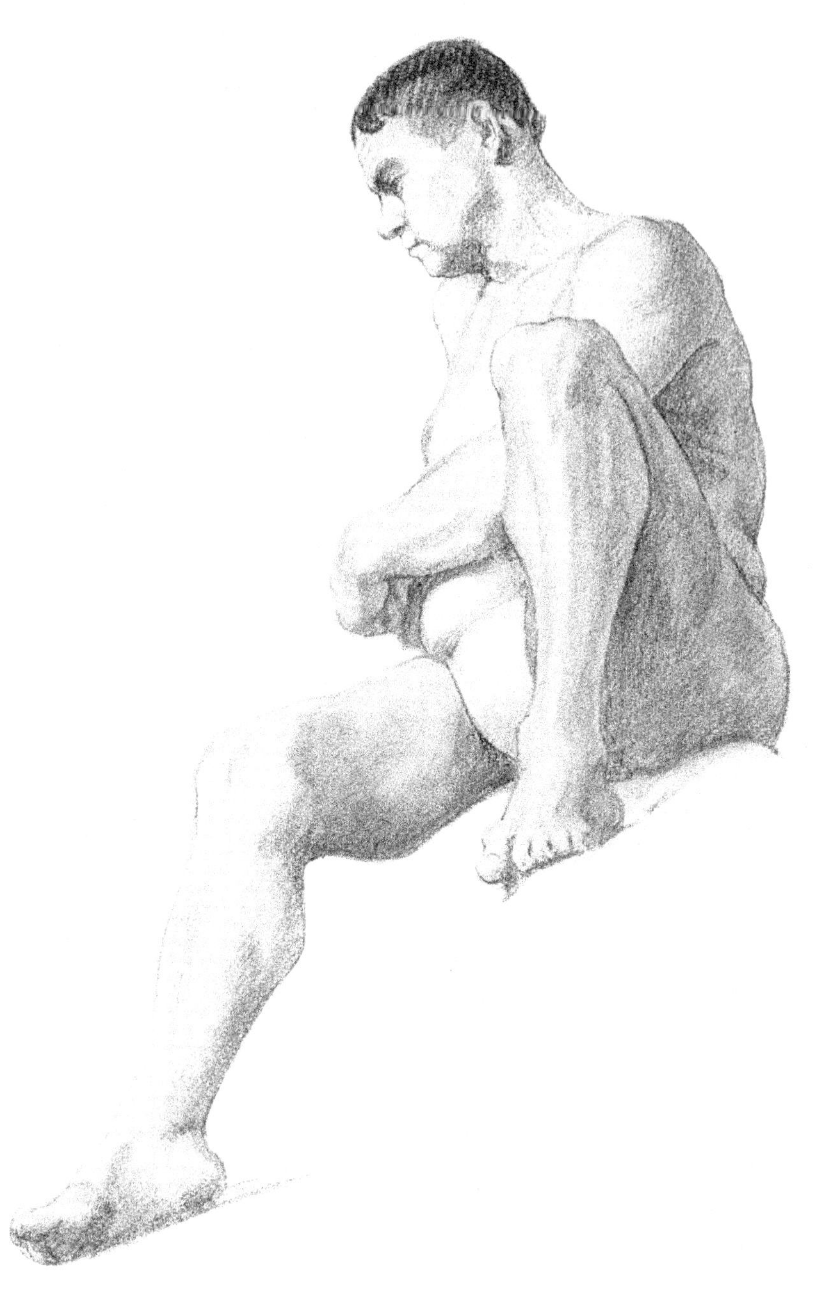

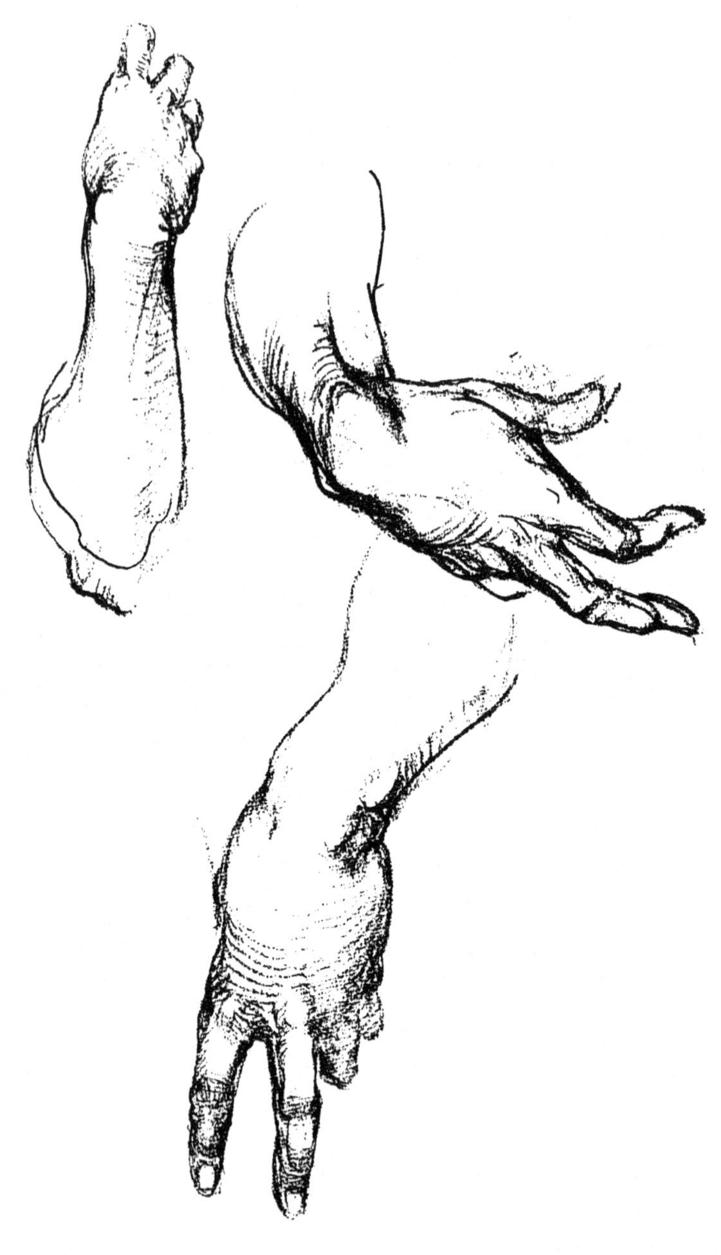

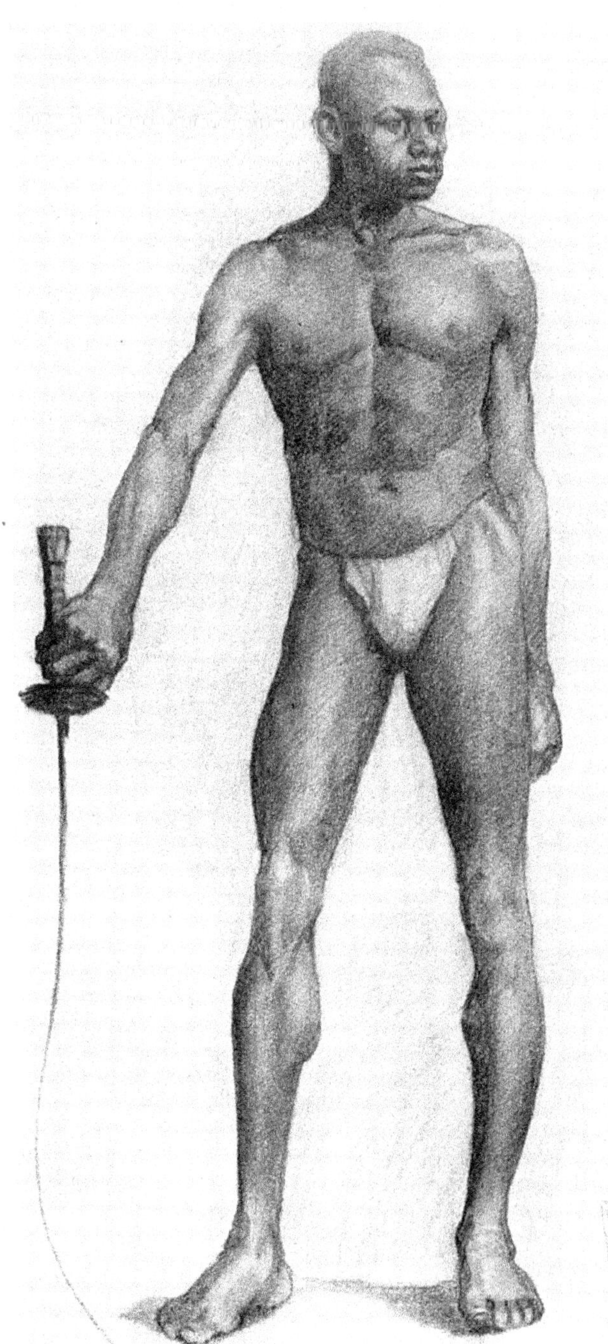

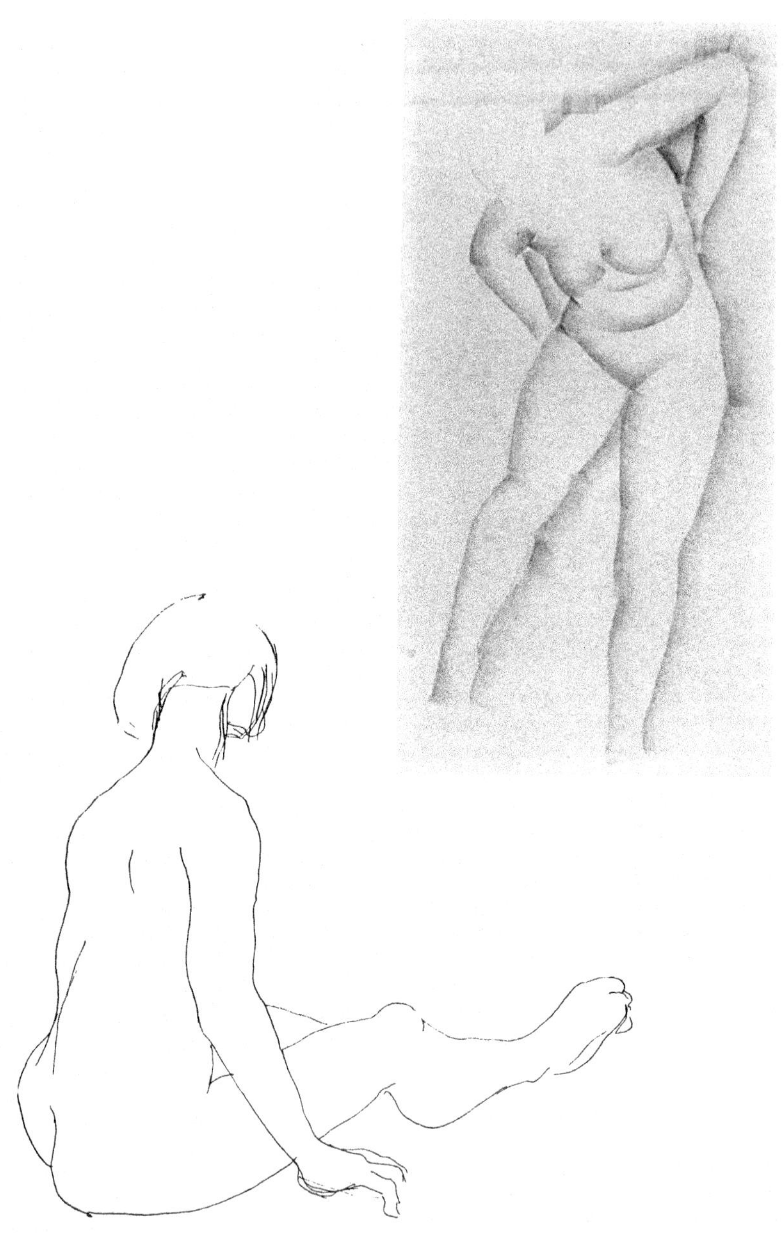

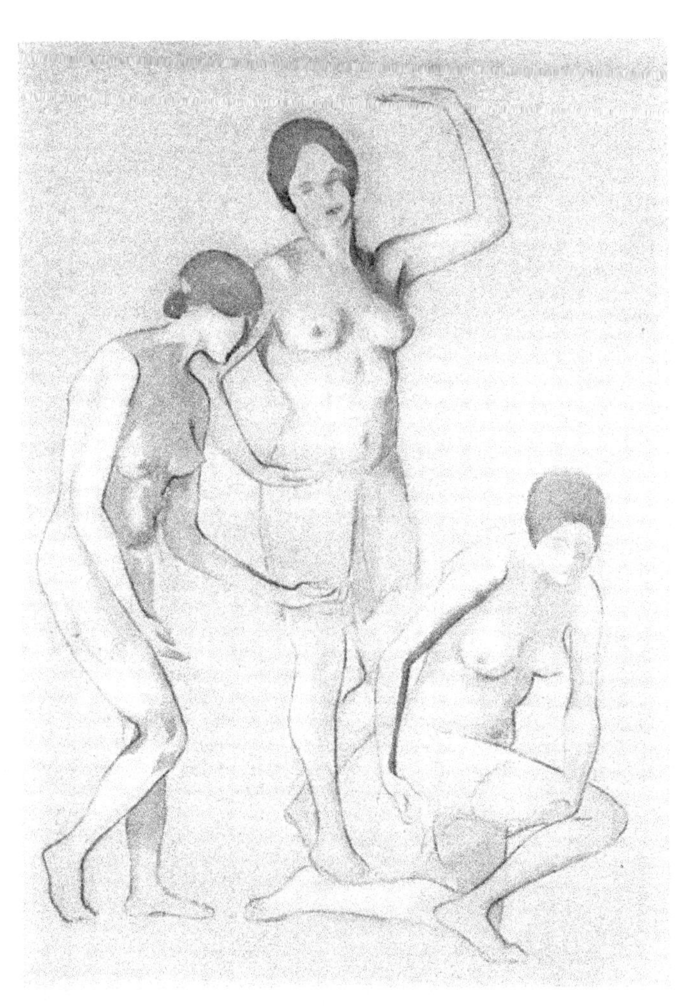

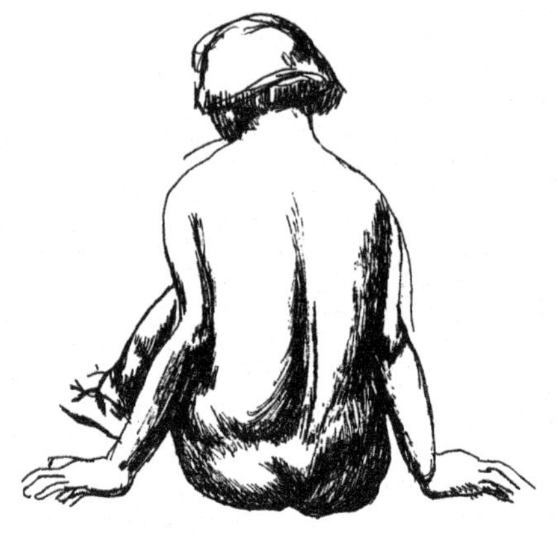

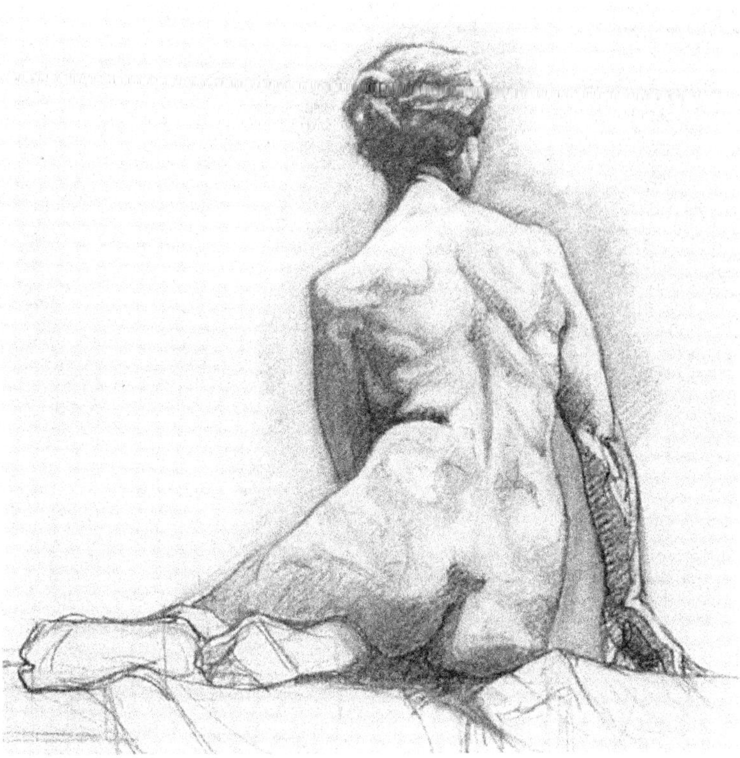

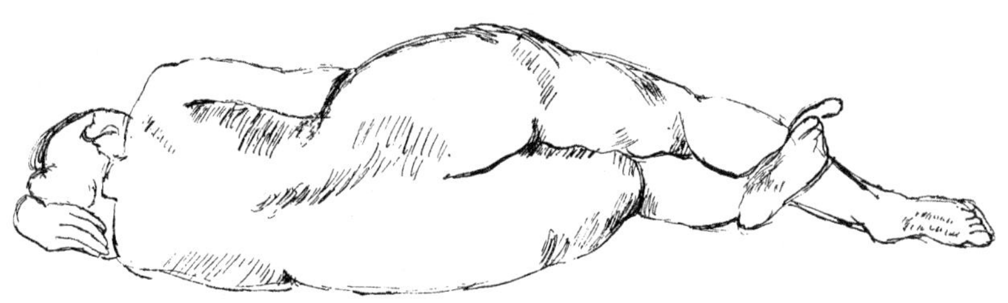

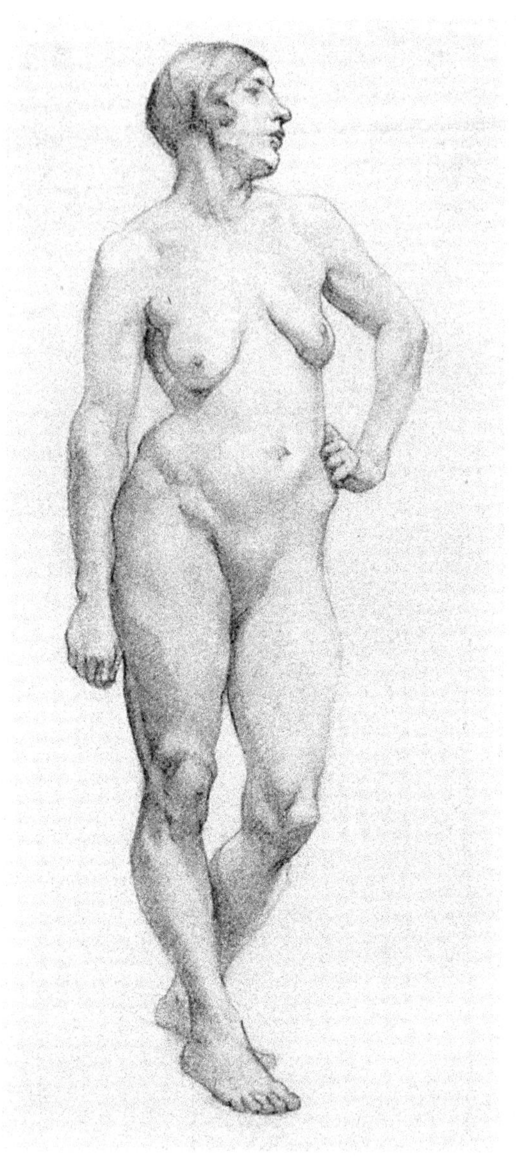

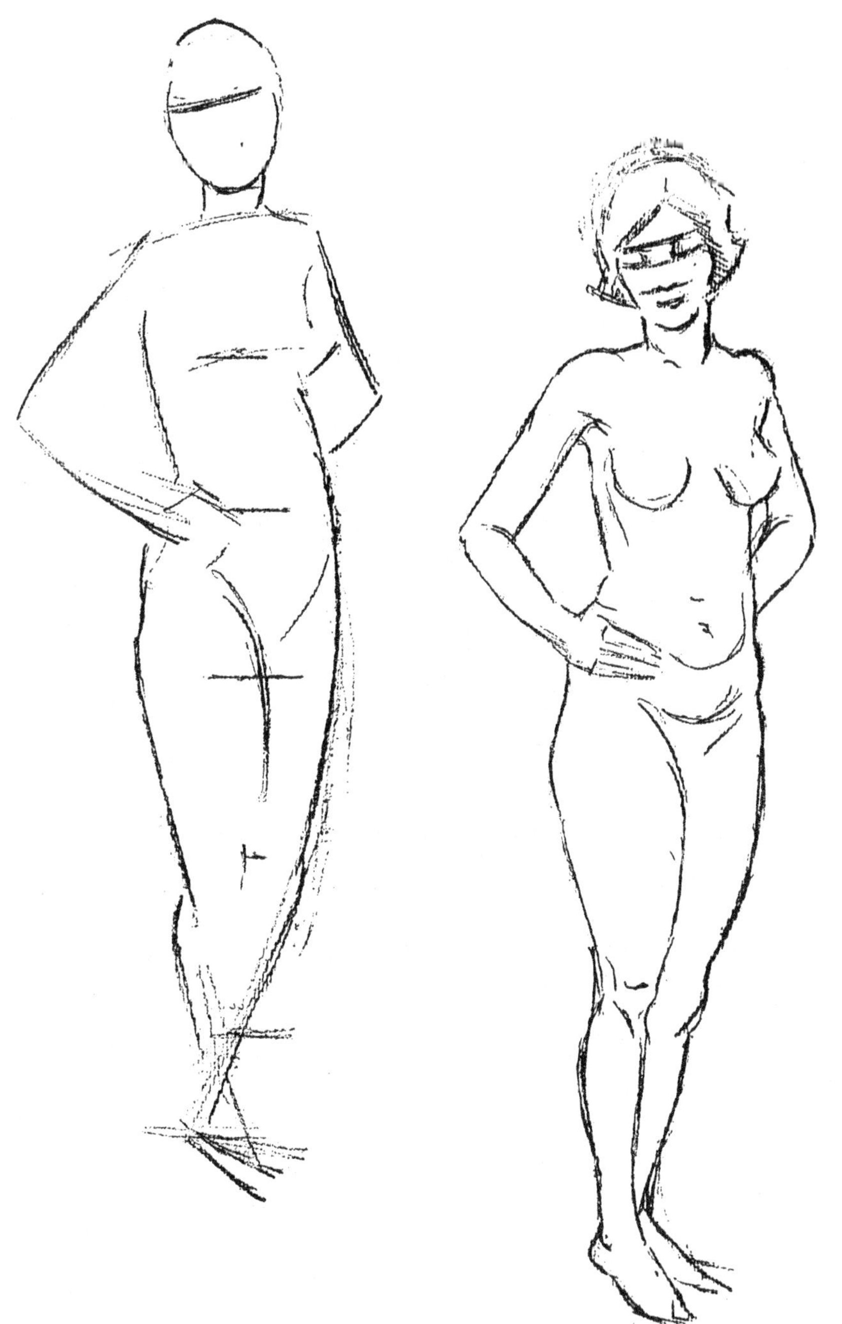

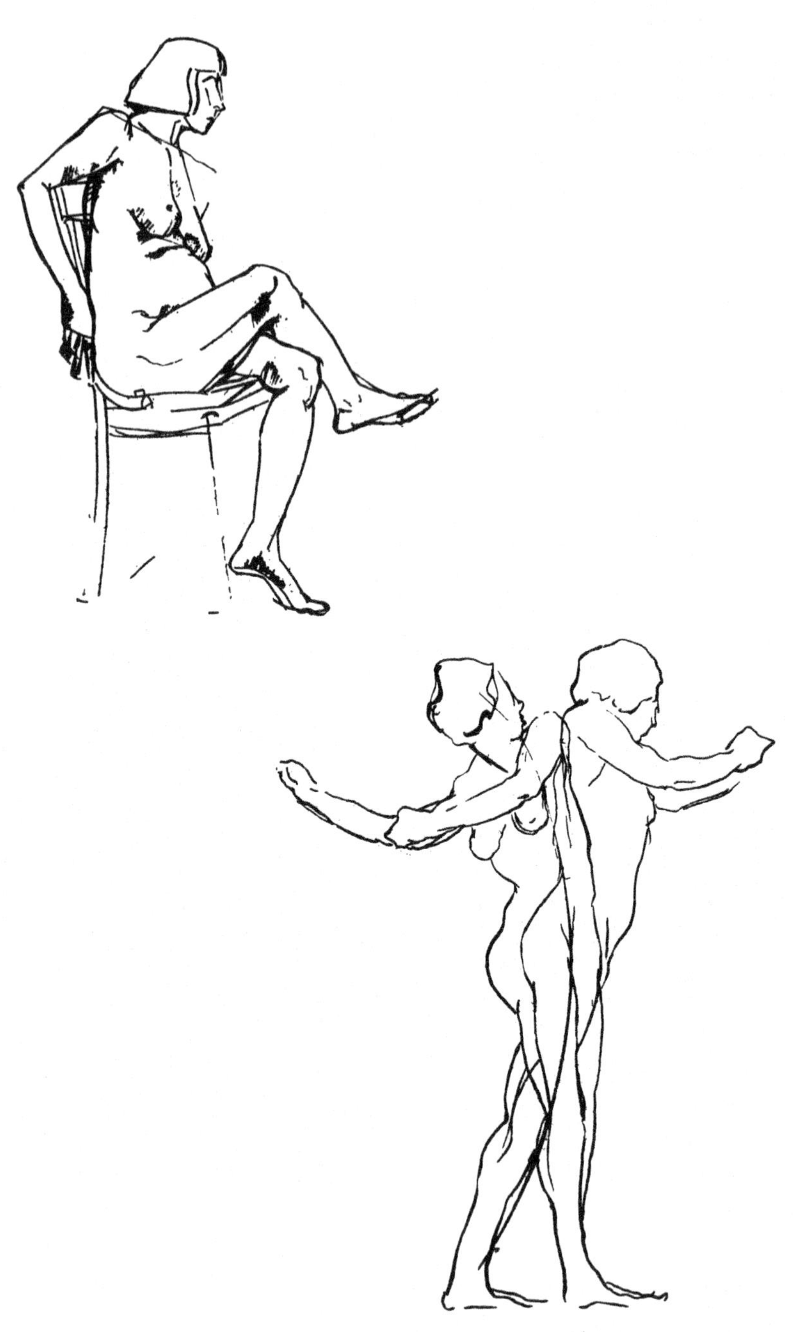

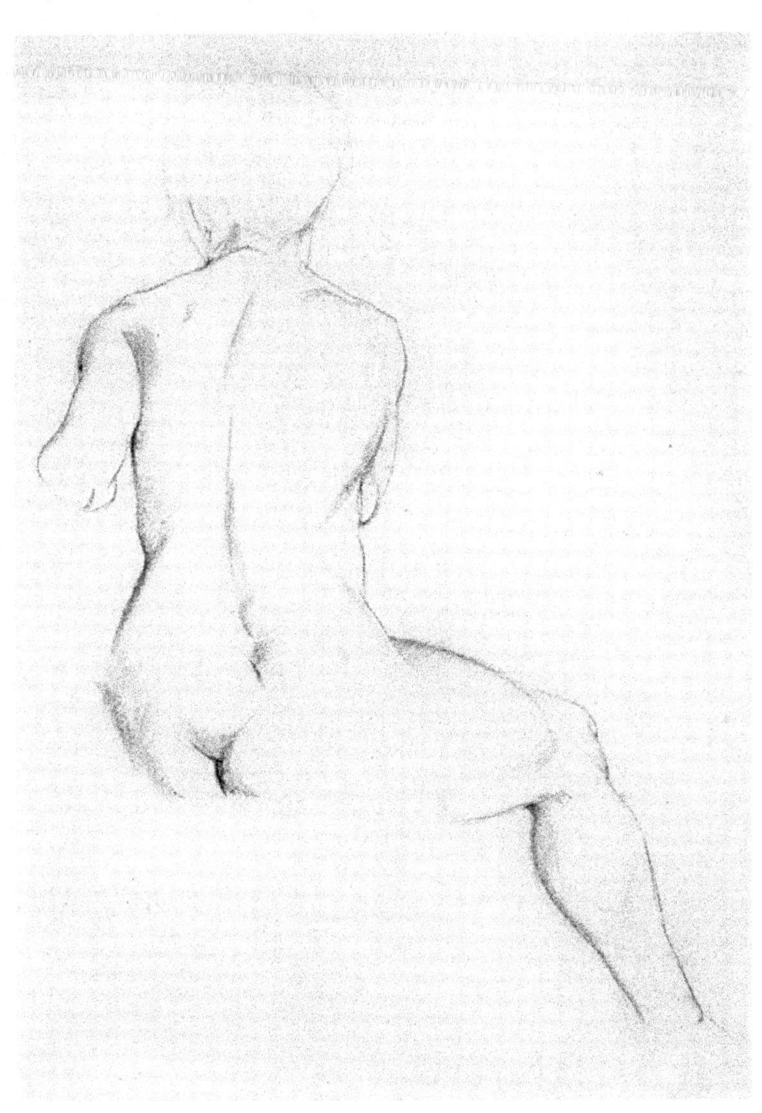

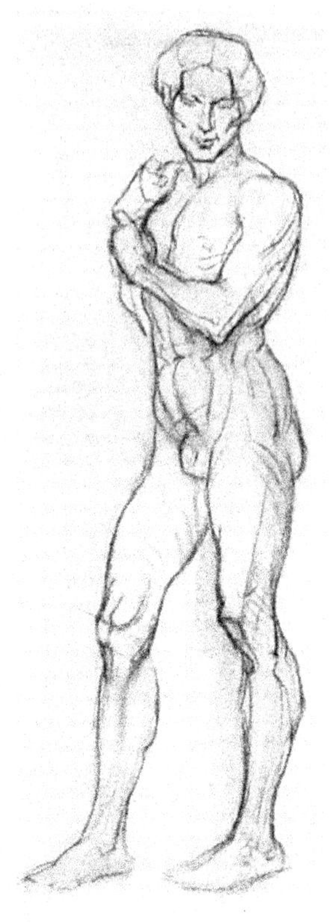

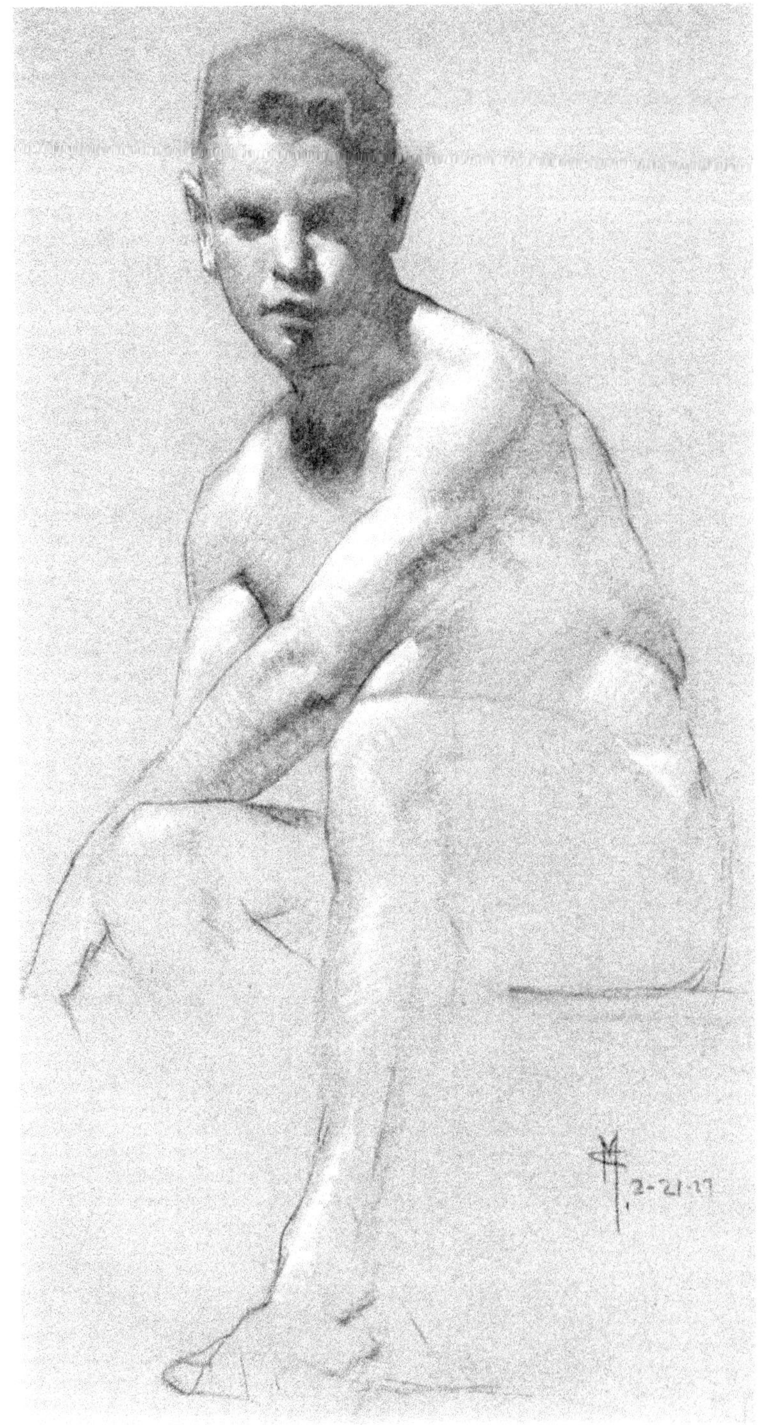

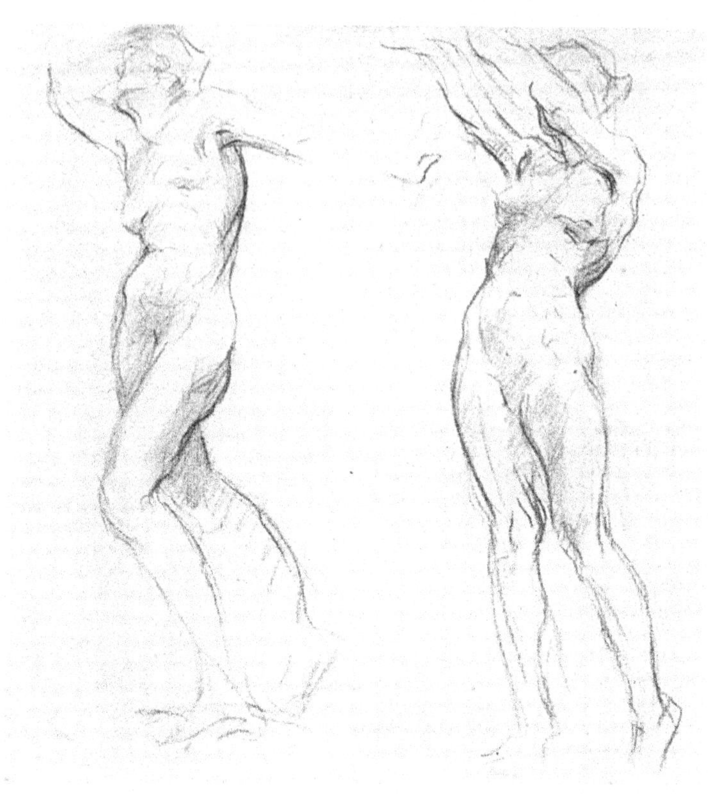

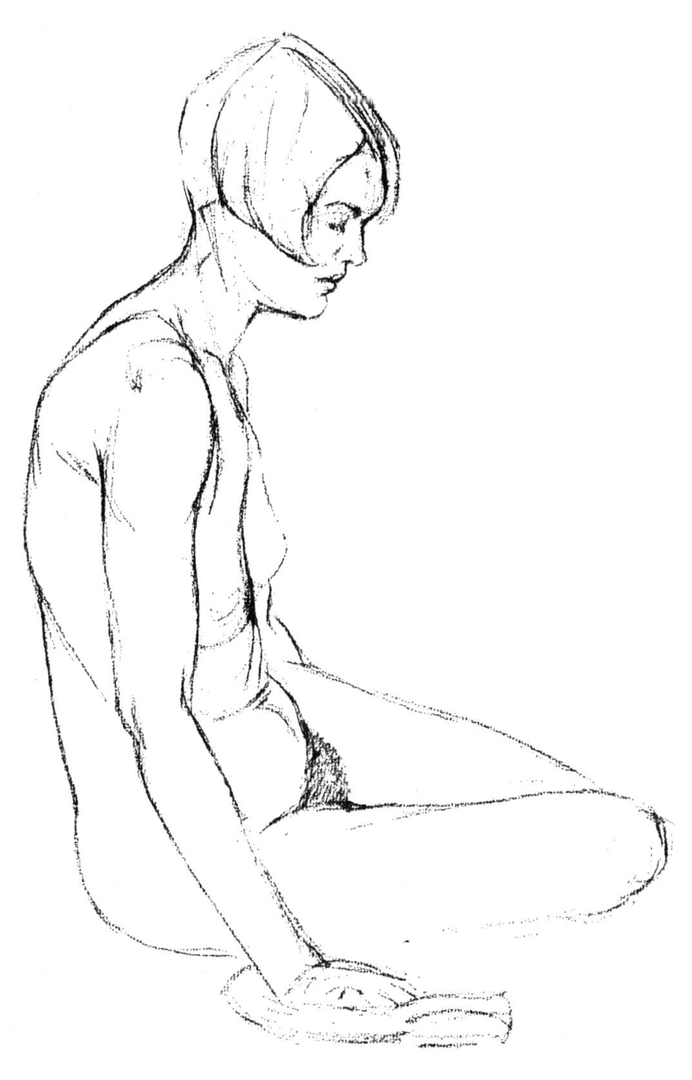

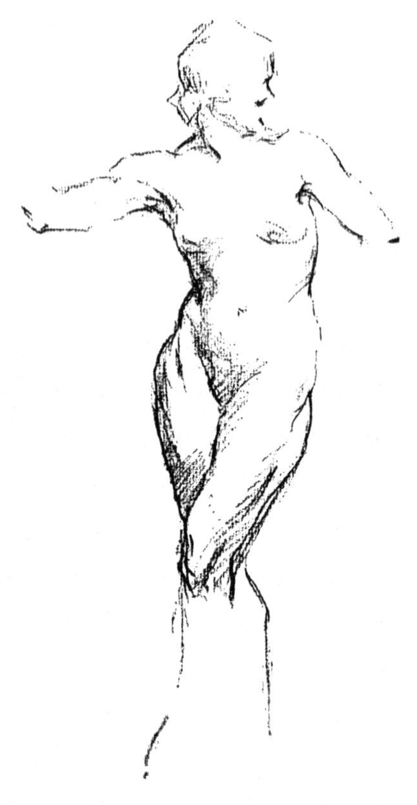

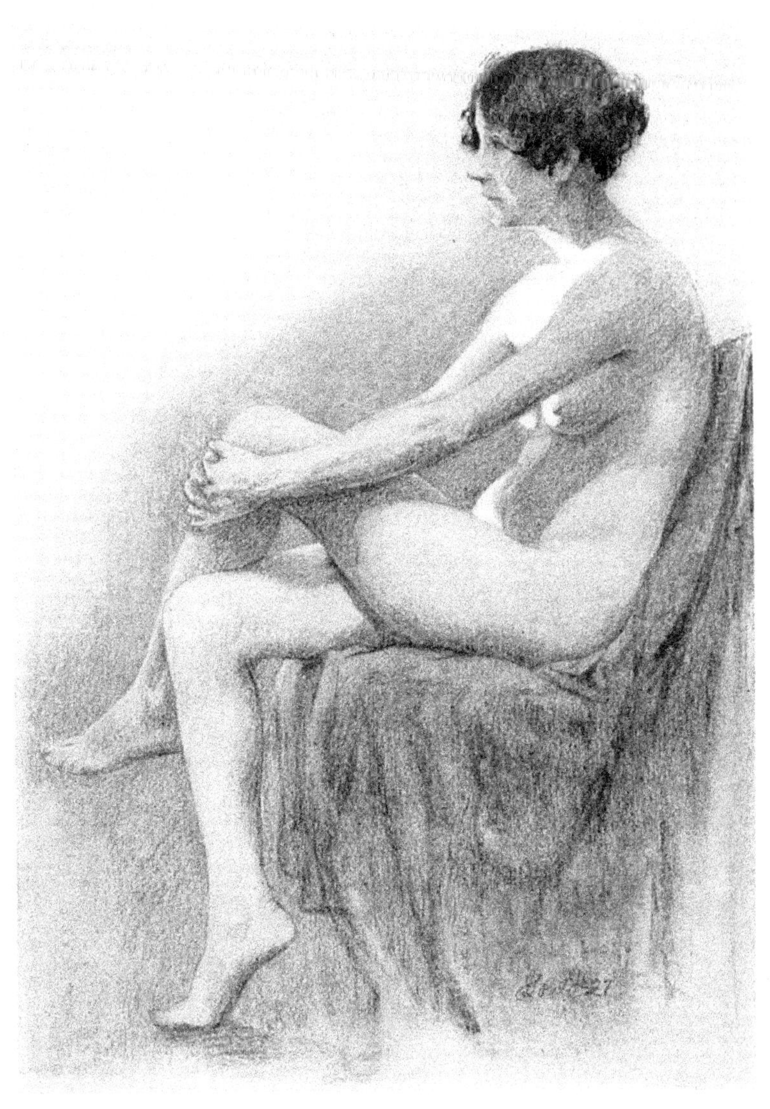

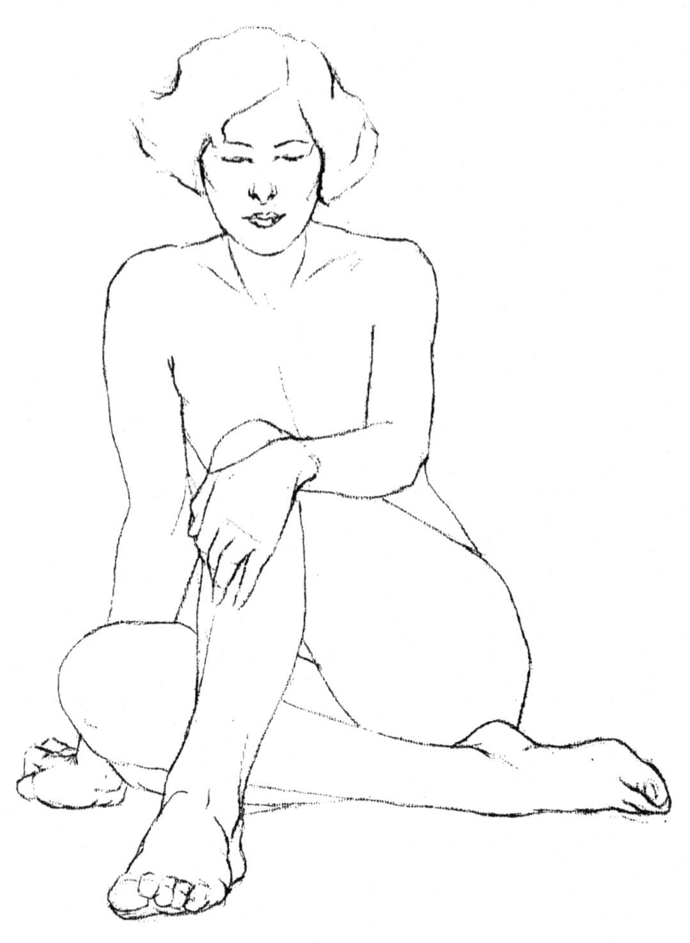

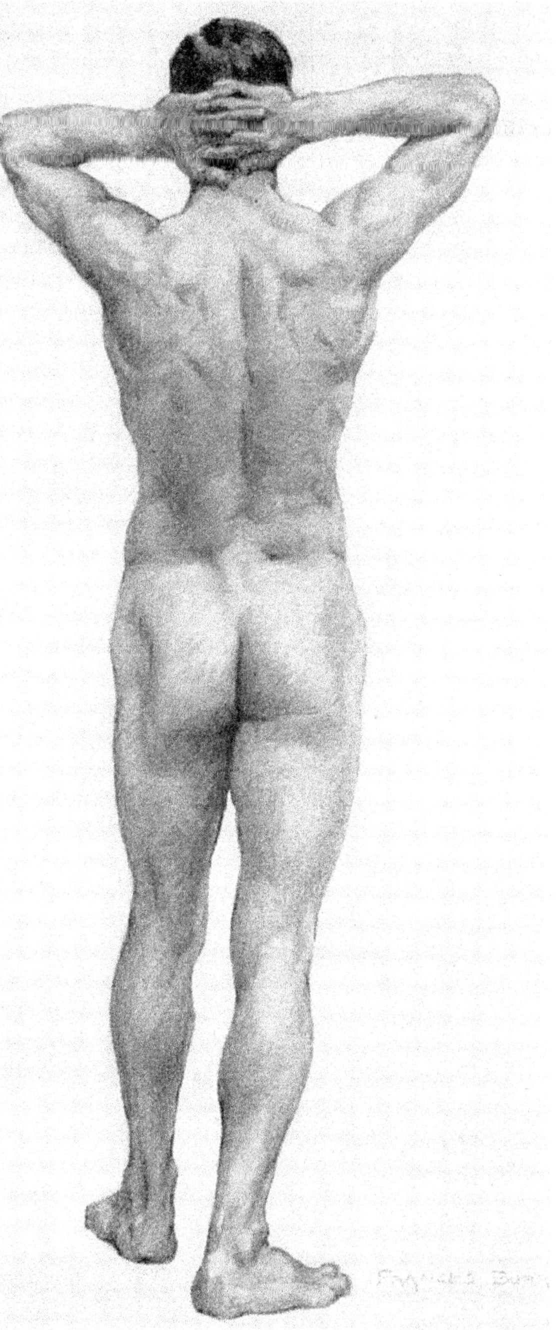

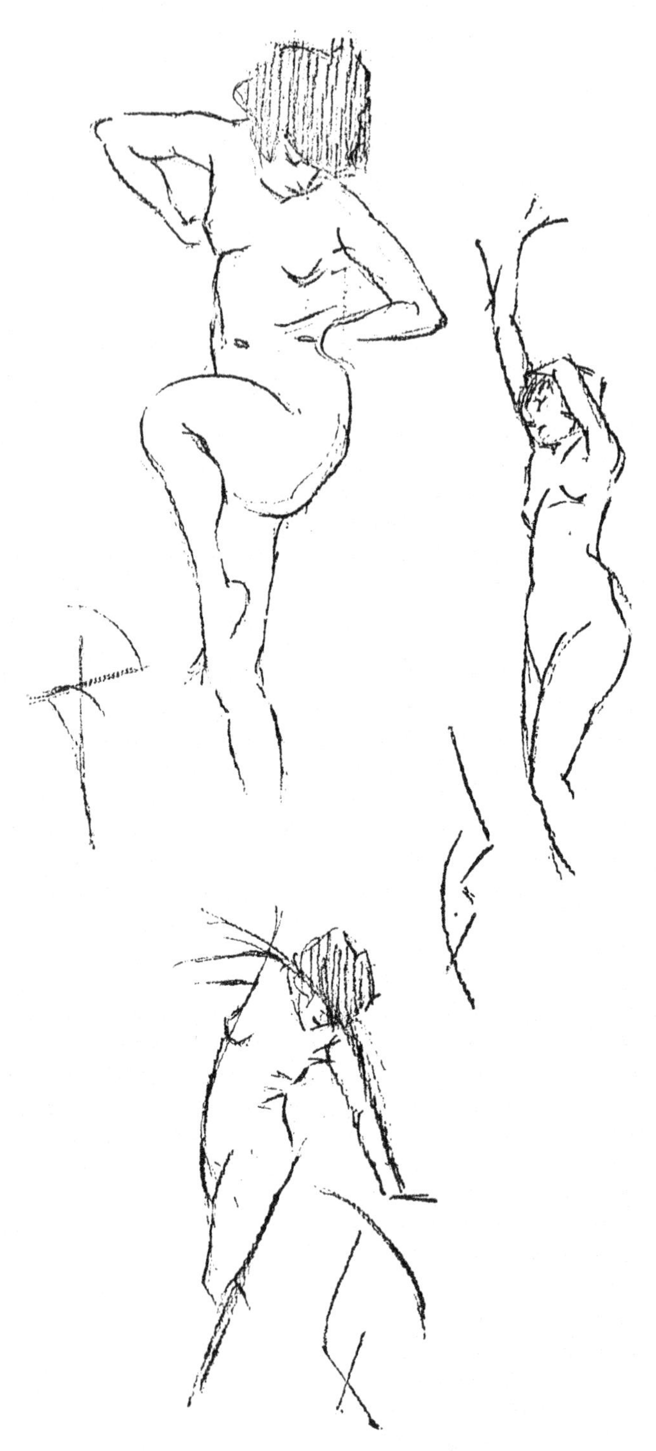

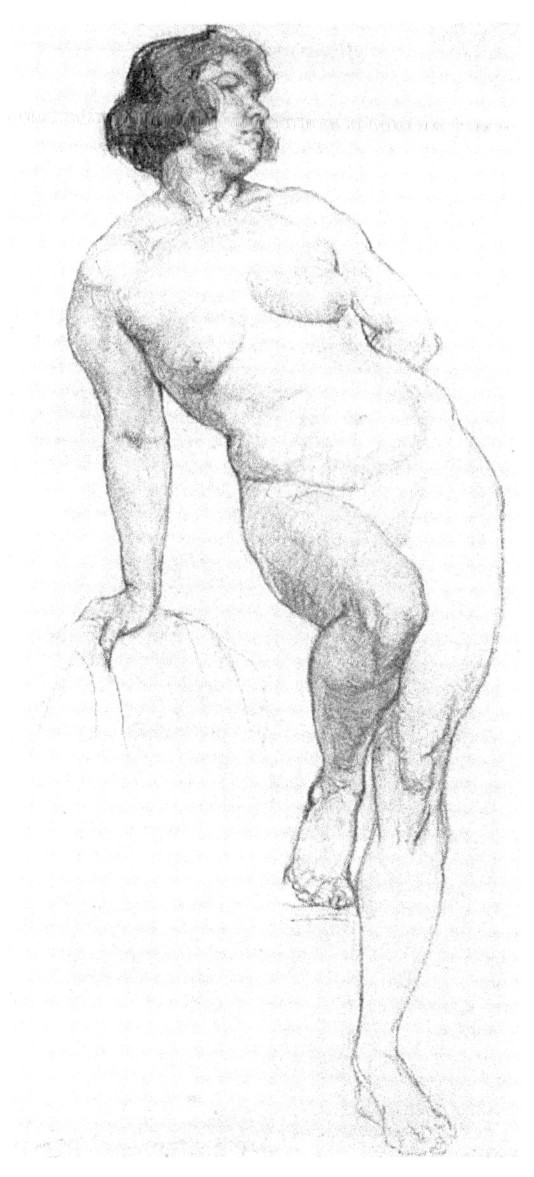

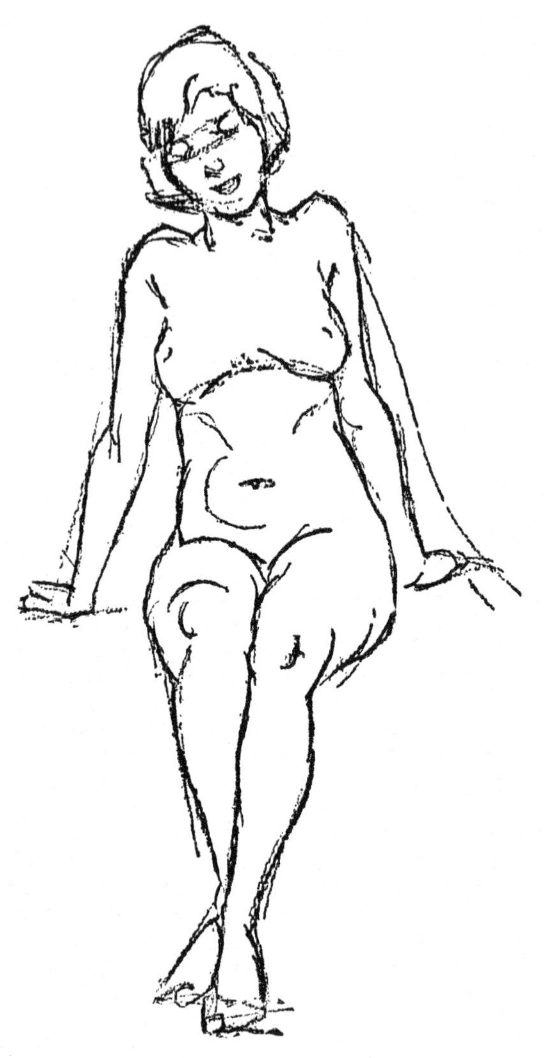

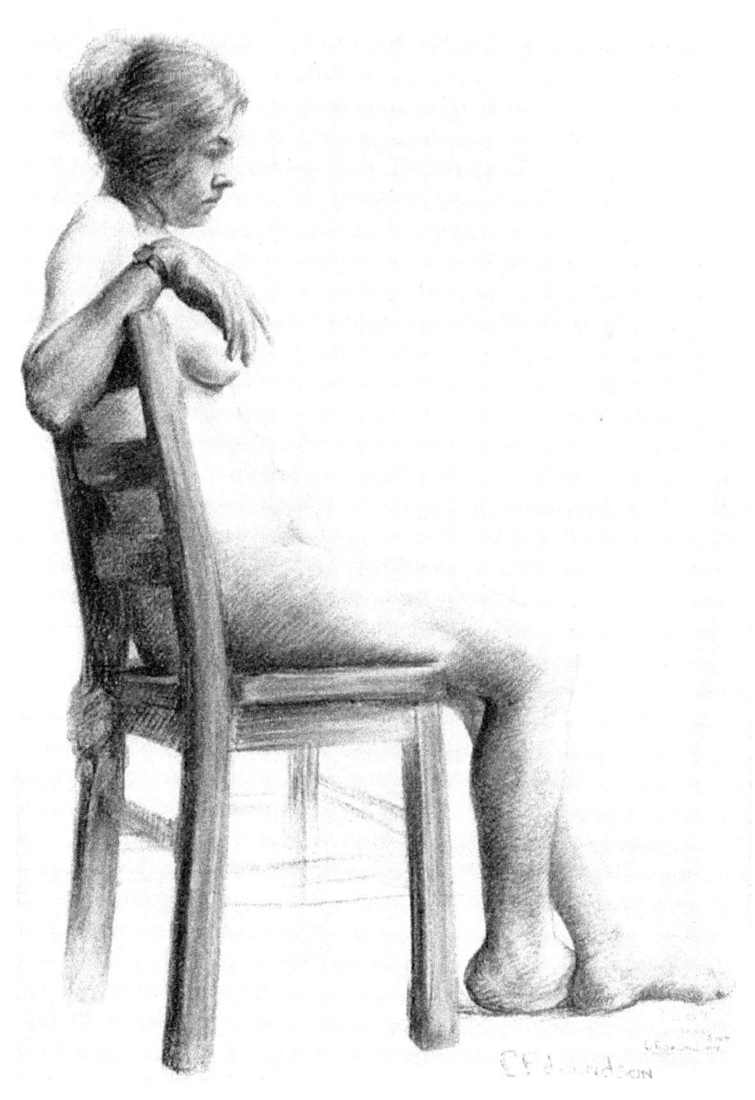

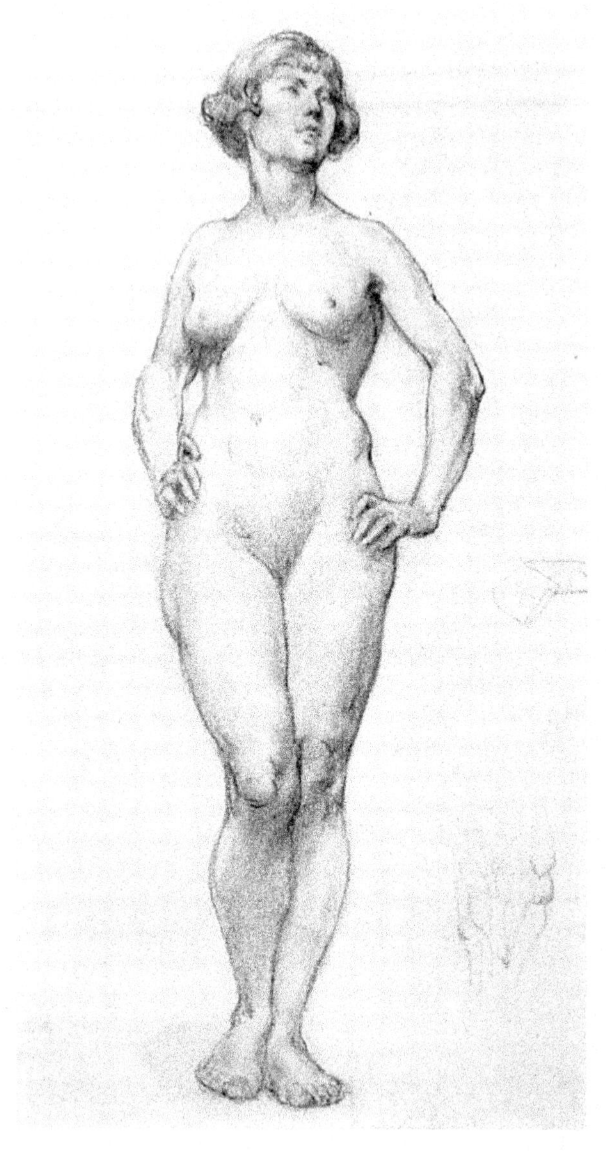

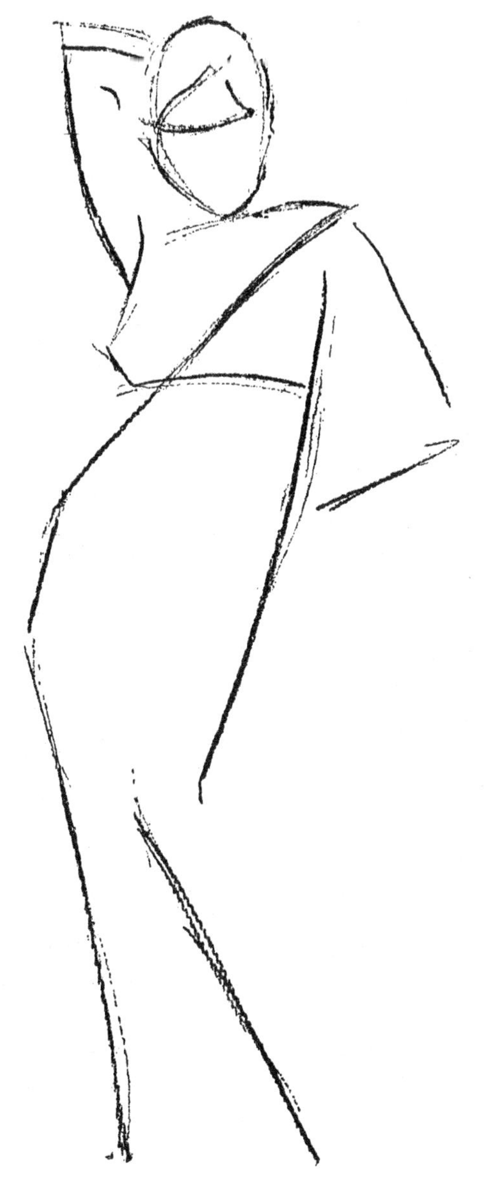

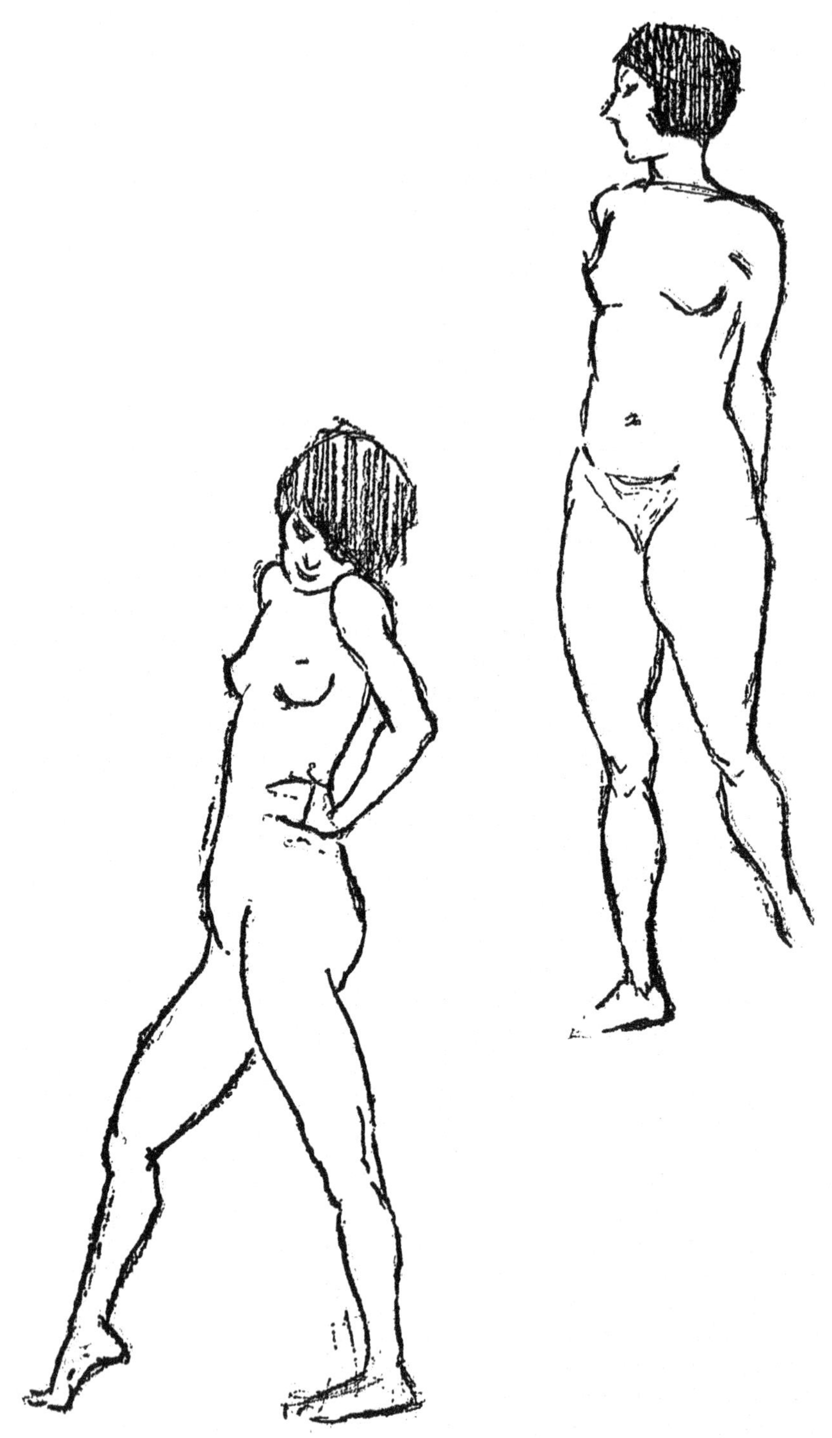

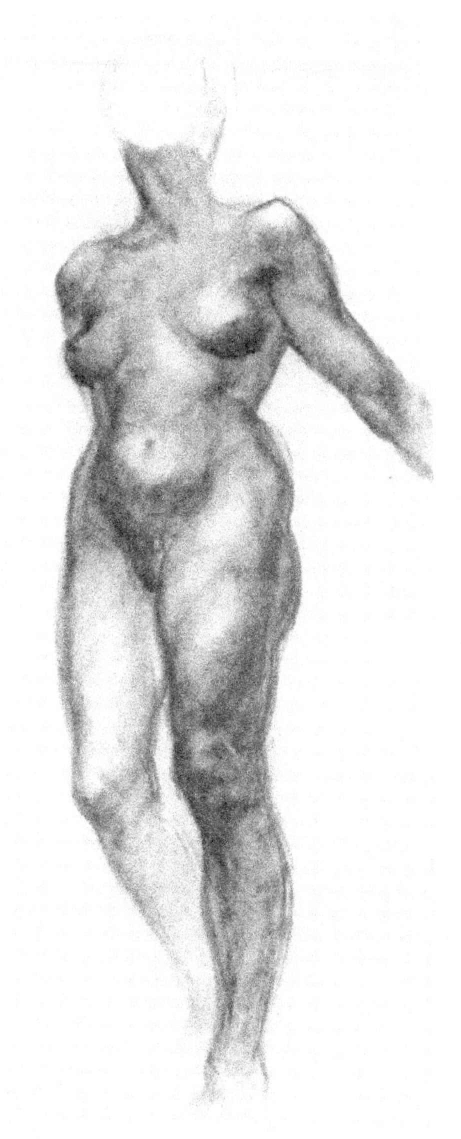

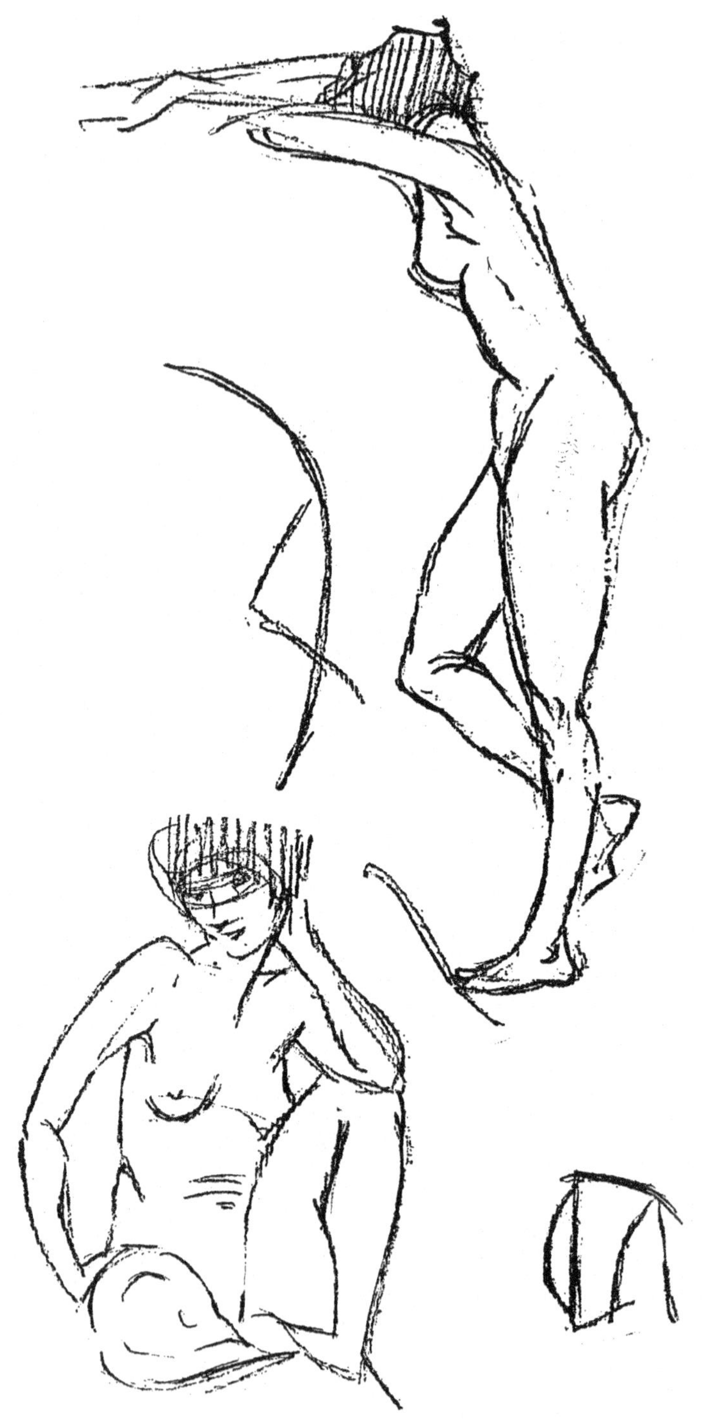

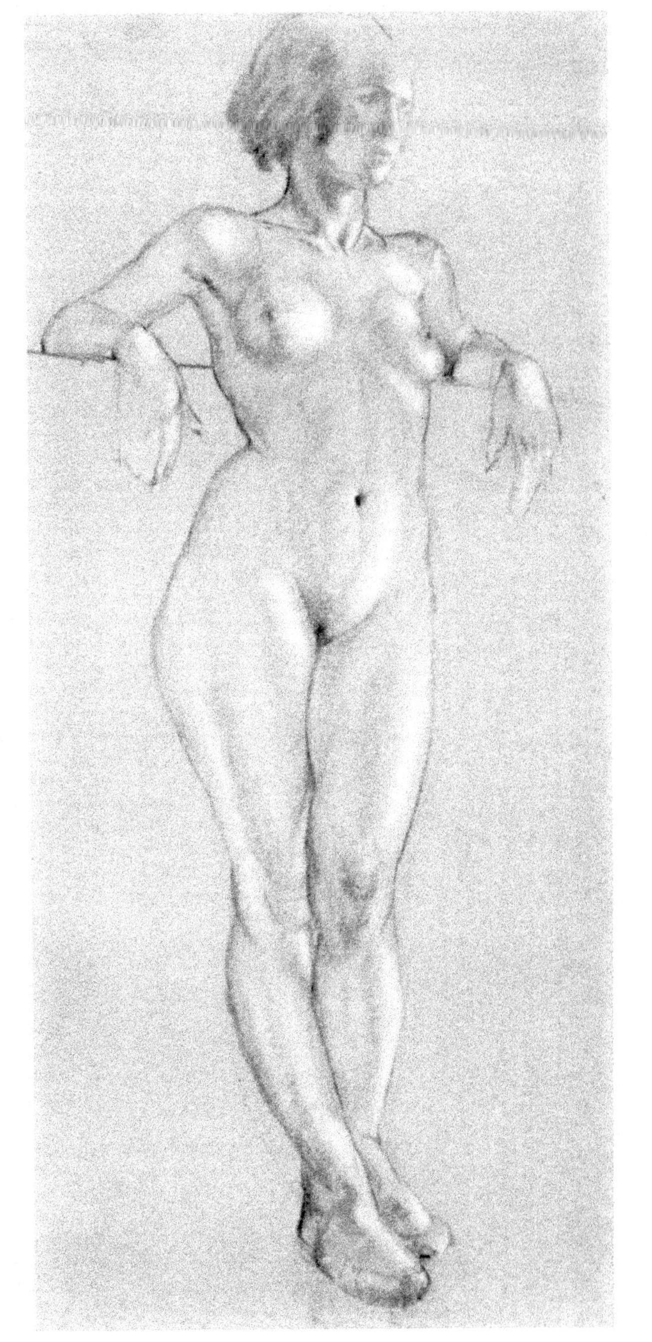

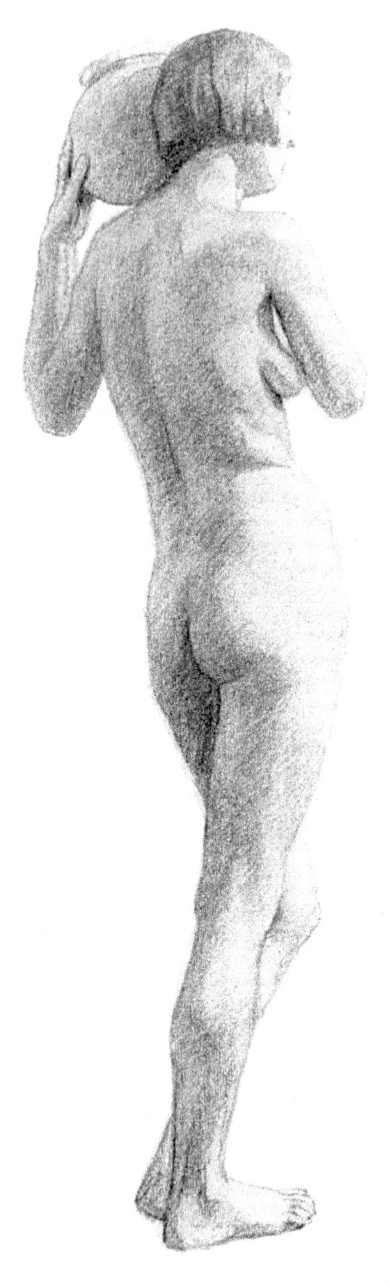

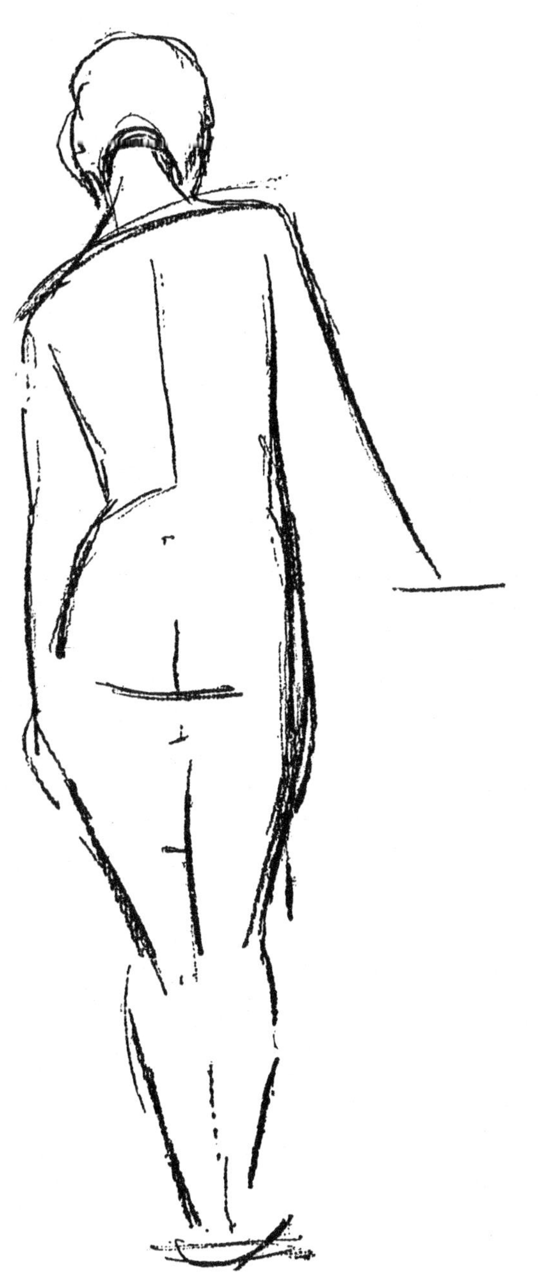

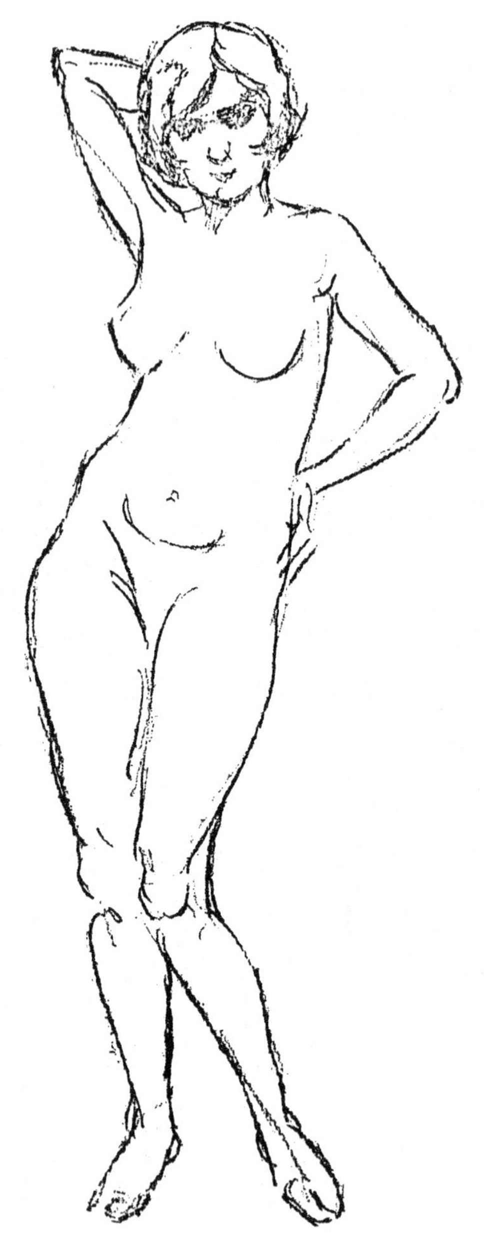

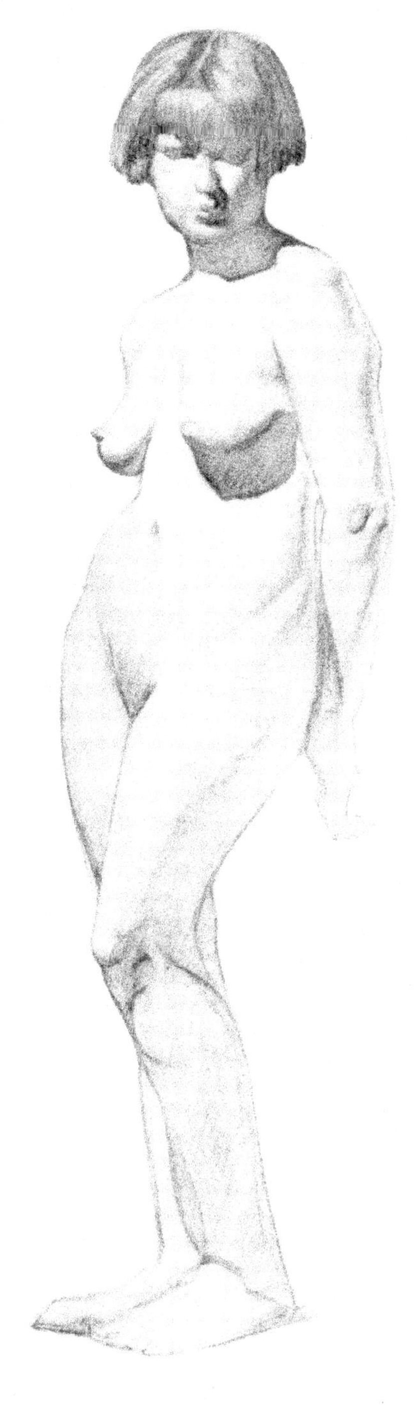

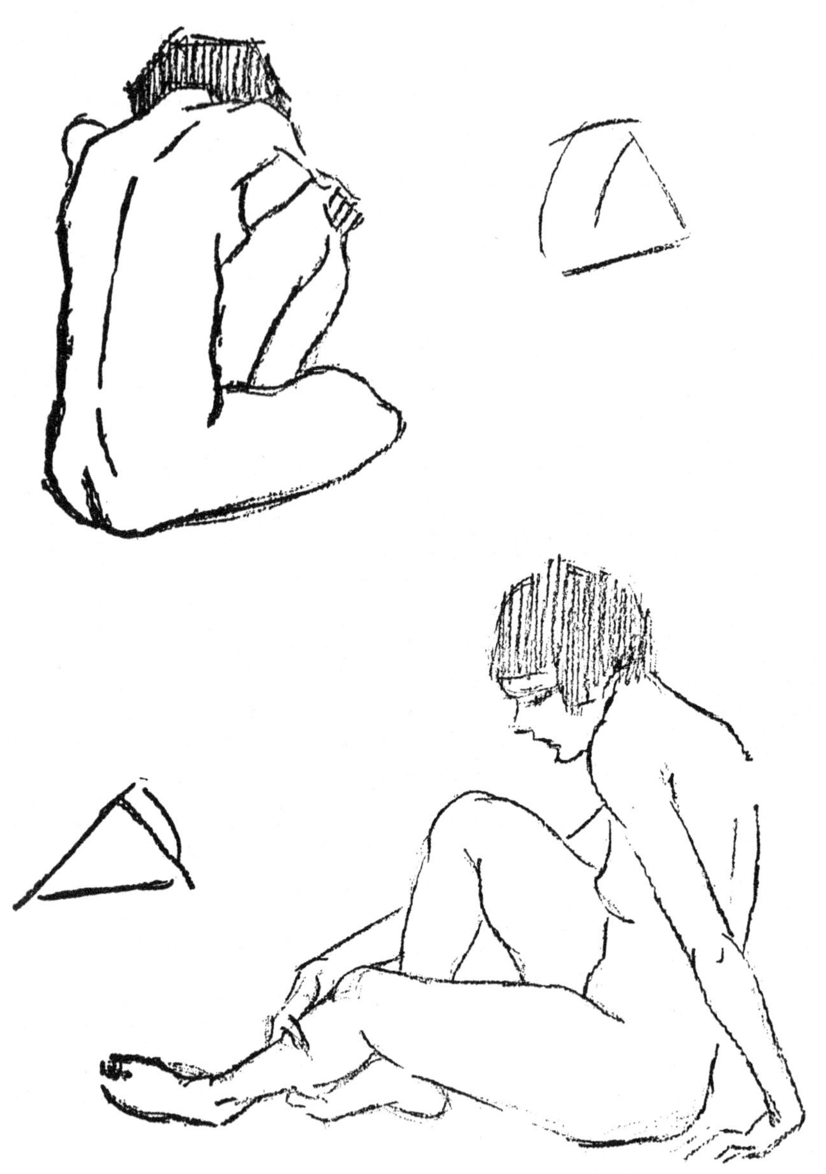

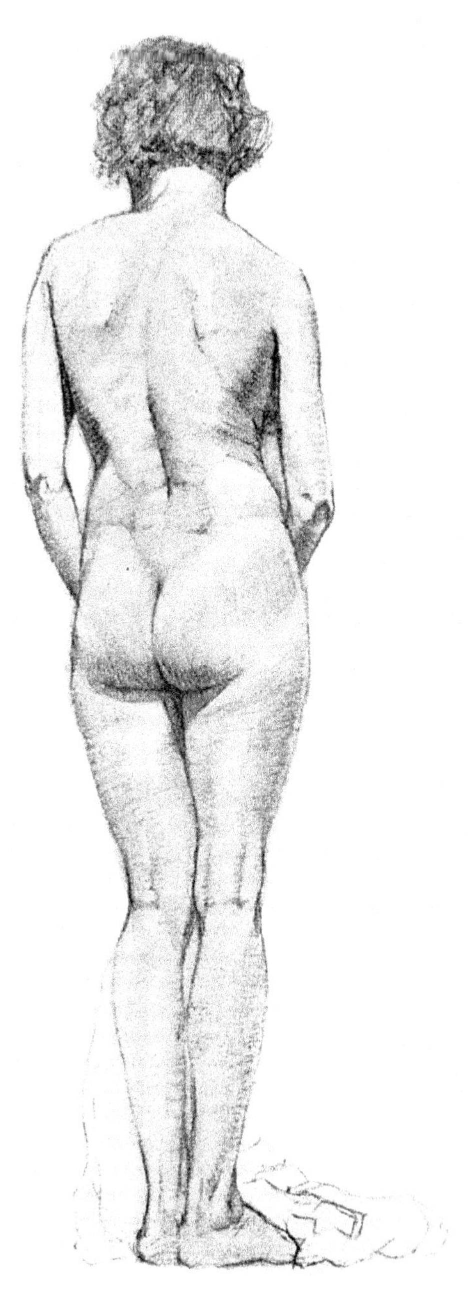

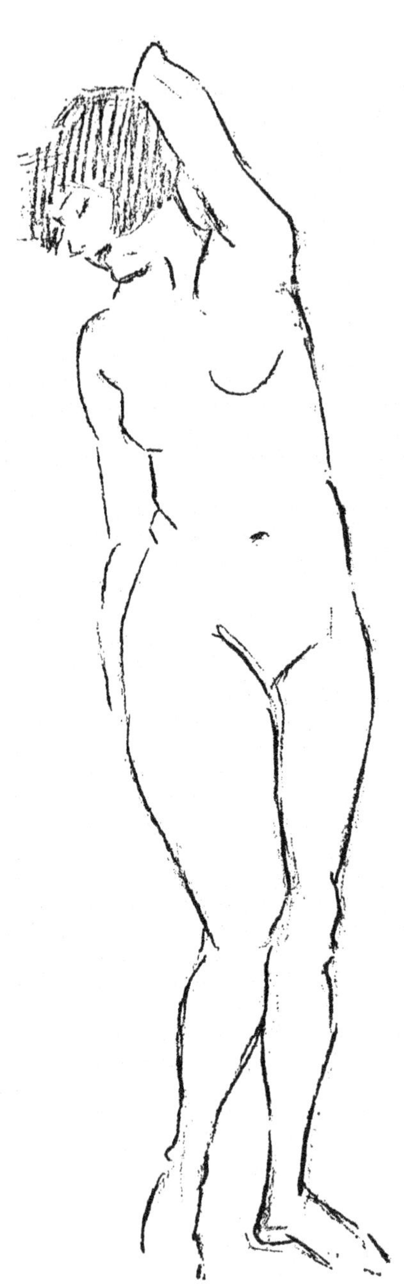

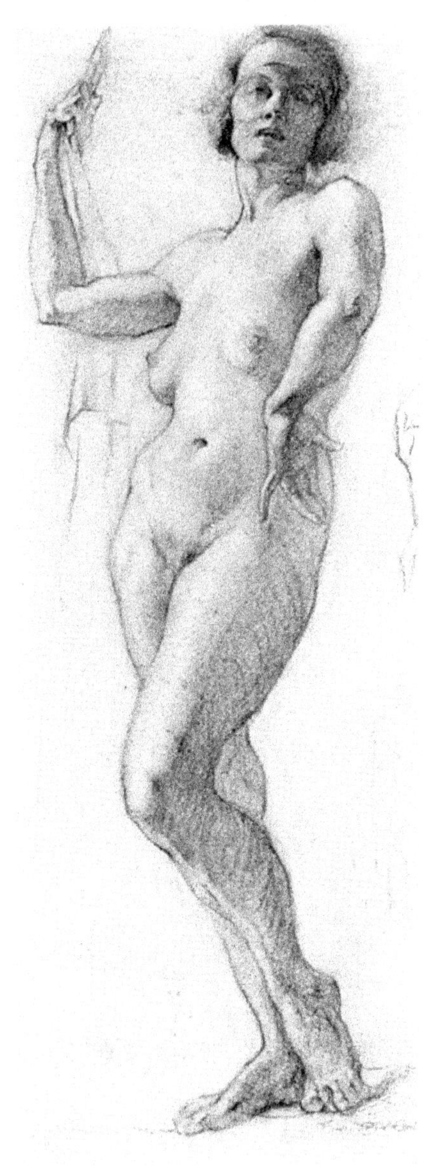

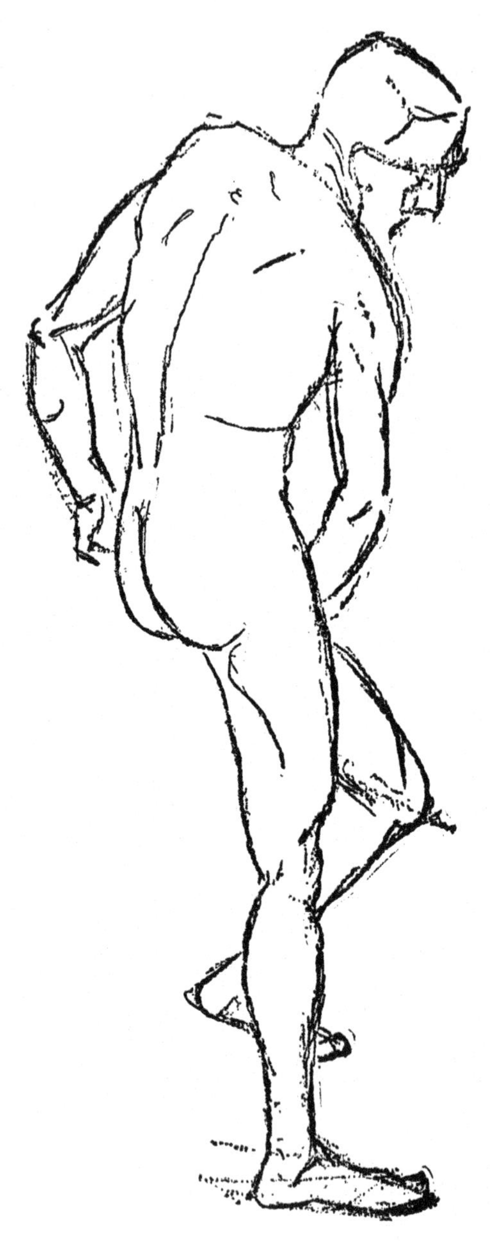